MONARCHY IN THE TWENTIETH CENTURY

MONARCHY
IN THE TWENTIETH
CENTURY

Sir Charles Petrie, Bt.

M.A. (Oxon). F.R.Hist.S., Corresponding Member of the
Royal Spanish Academy of History

LONDON
ANDREW DAKERS LIMITED

First Published 1952

*Set in 12/13 pt. Baskerville and made and printed in Great Britain by
John Gardner (Printers) Ltd., Liverpool 20*

Le métier de Roi est grand, noble, et délicieux

LOUIS XIV

CONTENTS

PART ONE

I

POSITION OF THE MONARCHY AT THE DEATH OF QUEEN VICTORIA

Feudalism and the Corporate State—The Crown during the Wars of the Roses—The New Monarchy and the Policy of Henry VIII—The Earlier Stuarts—The Commonwealth and the Triumph of Faction—The National Monarchy of Charles II—The Revolution of 1688—Bolingbroke and the Patriot King—Revival of the Crown under George III—The Reigns of George IV and William IV—Decline of the Royal Power under Queen Victoria—The Rise and Fall of the Republican Movement

ON JANUARY 22nd, 1901, there took place the death of Queen Victoria, who had ascended the throne in 1837, and thus came to an end the longest reign in English history. Even at the time it was widely felt that this event marked the termination of one epoch, and the commencement of another, a feeling which was accentuated by the fact that a new century had just begun. For once a contemporary estimate has proved to be more than usually accurate, and as the year 1901 is a definite milestone in the national history it will be as well to begin this study of the British monarchy by examining its position at that date. First of all, however, it is necessary to look back in order the better to realize how this position had been reached, and for this purpose the evolution of the monarchy since the Middle Ages must be briefly traced.

English kingship had its roots in Feudalism, which was not so much a form of government in the ordinarily accepted sense of the term as a form of civilization. The Feudal State was essentially a Corporate State.

Representation was by interests and by occupation, rather than by the counting of heads grouped together upon a geographical basis for the purpose of an election. The so-called Model Parliament, convoked by Edward I in 1295, provides an excellent illustration of this. There came together on that occasion the great spiritual and lay peers in person; the representatives of the lower clergy; two knights from each shire; and a varying number of members, generally two, from each town and borough. The lower clergy, it is true, soon preferred to sit in Convocation by themselves, and this proved to be the first step in the direction of representation by geography rather than by interests. At the end of the thirteenth century there were only three occupations of any importance in the country, namely those of agriculturalist, trader, and priest, and they were all duly represented in the Model Parliament. The landed interest spoke through the mouths of the lay peers and of the knights of the shire; trade and industry were represented by the borough members; while the bishops, mitred abbots, and the nominees of the lower clergy stood for the Church and its interests. It is true that the constituencies were divided geographically, but the reason is that in those days the economic and geographical divisions were the same, for the primitive means of transport at his disposal prevented the London merchant from having his domicile in some rural district of Hertfordshire or Sussex.

At the apex of this pyramid stood the monarch, the symbol of the nation as a whole, and as the representative of which he was, after his coronation, the Lord's anointed. He was not a despot, bound by no laws other than those of his own making; rather was he an integral part of the system of which he was the head. His crown was the emblem of his trusteeship for his people, and his rights and duties were as exactly defined as those of his subjects. That was, indeed, the distinguishing characteristic of Feudalism: every man and woman had a definite place in society, which was responsible to them as they were to it. There were penalties attaching to neglect of these responsibilities, and from them even the King was not exempt. At the same time he was no figure-head, like the Doge of Venice, for an incompetent monarch, such as Stephen, meant a relapse into that anarchy which the Feudal System had been established to prevent.

On the whole this state of affairs worked well until the middle of the fourteenth century, when the Black Death shook the economic and social foundations upon which Feudalism rested. In addition, there was the general disturbance of society occasioned by the Hundred Years' War, and in these circumstances it is not surprising that the period which followed was one of continuous civil disorder, mitigated only by the short reign of Henry V. The real cause, however, of the chaotic condition into which England relapsed at this time was that the Crown became merely the head of one of the contending parties in the State. The later years of Edward III were marked by growing weakness at the centre, and Richard II was too young when he succeeded to the throne to control the ambitions of his relatives; in the last decade of his reign he made such an effort, but he appears to have been deficient in that tact which is so essential an adjunct to successful statesmanship: however this may be, the forces arrayed against him proved too strong, and he was overthrown. Thereafter, for a century, the monarch was no more than a leader, or the puppet of the leaders, of one of the factions of the State. The Lancastrian

Experiment was an experiment, not only in Parliamentary, but also in what is so often its corollary, uncontrolled party, government, and the result was the anarchy of the Wars of the Roses. When they began, England was the leading Power in Europe; when they finished she was hardly even a makeweight.

The obscurity in which the reign of Henry IV is enveloped has not yet been completely penetrated by the historians of the period, but it is clear that until the day of his death his throne was by no means secure, and he depended upon a faction rather than upon the nation as a whole. Henry V thoroughly appreciated the weakness of such a position, and he deliberately revived the old claim to the French crown with a view to diverting public attention from domestic affairs: even so, he had to deal with at any rate one serious conspiracy, while it is impossible to say how far he might have succeeded, for his career was terminated by an early death. The reign of his son is an example of the dangers attendant upon a monarchy dominated by interests, instead of one that dominates them. Save possibly for a few weeks in 1459, when, incidentally, he carried all before him, Henry VI never acted on his own initiative, and the possession of his person in order to give an appearance of legality to their proceedings became the object of the contending parties. Finally, the Yorkists raised their own leader to the throne, and thereafter the victory of one faction or the other meant a change of monarch.

The continued prevalence of political unrest during this period was the consequence of the weakness of the throne, and the result of the Wars of the Roses was to impress this fact upon the mass of the English people, so that for two centuries the monarch could always rely upon their support in his struggle against the parties. The personal appeal of Mary I to the citizens of London for aid against Wyatt is typical of the national support that was forthcoming for the Crown when the occupant of the throne knew how to invoke it. Those who would question this statement would do well to remember that the government of those days had not at its disposal the vast resources that a modern administration wields. There was no standing army and no police force to overawe its opponents, and the monarch had not in his gift innumerable lucrative offices with which to buy off the most dangerous of his critics. He could, it is true, confer titles, but hardly sell them, for ready money was scarce, and as the ennoblement of a man still meant to increase his importance it was a dangerous step to take with any of whose loyalty there was the least doubt. A few archers and men-at-arms, hardly sufficient to defend the palace against sudden attack, were all the force upon which Henry VII could absolutely rely, and the secret of the strength of what is termed the New Monarchy must be sought elsewhere.

The strong government of Edward IV, Richard III, and the Tudors represented the triumph of the nation over the factions, and the nation was symbolized by the Crown. There were occasions when a relapse was threatened, but it never actually took place, and the parties were controlled by the throne, instead of controlling it as they had done for so long. That Henry VII to some extent, and his son most certainly, was ruthless in his methods cannot be denied, but after the failure of Perkin Warbeck no rebellion against either had any real chance of success. The memory of the Wars of the Roses was so vivid that it seemed preferable to the ordinary citizen to bear with one tyrant than to be subject to the caprices of fifty, and so the Tudors kept the headsman busy without thereby rousing public opinion against them to any marked extent. In any event, until religious complications were added to the country's other problems, they struck at the class which had caused all the trouble for three generations, and in most instances had their victims succeeded in their projects it would only have been the old story of the Wars of the Roses over again. Such being the case, the nation had little sympathy for them or for their ambitions.

In the fourth decade of the sixteenth century there came the Reformation, and in retrospect we can see that this movement marked the turning-point in the history of the English monarchy. The clue to the Revolution is to be found in the Reformation, and to arrive at a true interpretation of the one it is first of all necessary to understand the other.

Many Catholic writers are inclined to place the emphasis upon the democratic doctrines of Protestantism, and to argue that it was these which weakened the monarchies of Europe in those countries that turned their backs on the old faith. That there is much in this theory cannot be denied, but it is not the whole truth, as the history of Prussia, Sweden, and Denmark serves to show, and it does not explain the course of events in seventeenth-century England. In effect, it was not so much the Reformation that weakened the English monarchy as the use which Henry VIII made of it.

The English Kings had always been suspicious of Papal encroachments, and Henry, in breaking with Rome, felt that he had freed the monarchy from that particular danger. However, the Tudor fear of the old nobility, which dated from the Wars of the Roses, when the Crown had been its plaything, caused Henry to raise up against the throne a far more formidable foe than the Pope had ever been, for the way in which he distributed the Church lands in due course created the Whig oligarchy. His intention was clearly to call into existence a class which should not only act as a counterpoise to the older magnates, but which, owing to the fear of losing the ecclesiastical property that it had acquired, could be relied upon to give steady support to the Crown in the struggle with Rome. In its immediate results this policy was justified, for Henry himself, Edward VI, and Elizabeth I were backed by the new nobility and gentry in their contests with the Papacy and Spain, but the price that the monarchy had to pay in the end was a very high one. Had Henry VIII kept the Church lands in his own possession, the Crown would have become so rich that, as in contemporary France, it could have afforded the luxury of a standing army, in which case the English Parliament might well have fallen into desuetude as did the French States-General. When it is remembered that in the last years of his reign Charles II, owing to the great increase in trade, found the revenue from the customs freed him to no inconsiderable extent from the dependence upon the House of Commons to which he had earlier been subjected, it is not difficult to appreciate what the position of the Crown might have been had it also had at its disposal the revenue from the confiscated possessions of the Church. In the new world that was coming into existence money was to be power in a way that it had not been in the less sophisticated days of the Feudal System.

So long as the threat from without, that is to say from Rome and Spain, continued to exist any anti-monarchical development was latent rather than potent, for even the most ambitious of the *nouveaux*

17

riches of the Reformation appreciated the fact that so far as the throne and himself were concerned, if they did not hang together, they would most assuredly hang separately. Furthermore, the first generation not only felt none too secure, but was also too busy in settling down, to feel disposed for political intrigue, while it rightly regarded the Crown as its chief defence against those who would rob it of its newly-won acres. In the reign of Elizabeth I this feeling was particularly strong, for those who regarded the new landowners as robbers also considered the Queen to be a bastard and a usurper, so that there was a remarkable similarity of outlook on the part of ruler and ruled. When, however, Philip II of Spain was dead, Mary Queen of Scots had been put out of the way, and there was clearly no danger of another Armada sailing up the Channel, the preliminary rumblings of the coming storm began to be heard, and Elizabeth in her last years felt the first gusts of that hurricane which in little more than a generation was to beat down everything before it.

When the Stuarts succeeded the Tudors the monarchy already contained within itself the seeds of that weakness which was to render it unequal to the performance of its old task of controlling the factions in the national interest. The chief cause of this weakness was its poverty. The value of money was steadily falling, and the price of wheat—a sure index—rose 250 per cent between 1570 and 1648. It had become impossible for the King to live on his own resources. Parliament, however, could not understand what was taking place, and it became increasingly suspicious of the Crown when it found that the money it voted was never enough to carry on the administration of the country. On the other hand, as always in a time of inflation, the possessors of land found themselves extremely well-placed, and they were the heirs of those who had done so well at the Reformation; they now filled the House of Commons and were everywhere dominant on the justice-bench. As Daniel Webster was to write two hundred years later, "There is not a more dangerous experiment than to place property in the hands of one class, and political power in those of another". Sooner or later the property will grasp at the political power, as in this particular instance the monarchy discovered to its cost.

The first monarch of the new dynasty, James I and VI, had as King of Scots proved one of the ablest rulers the northern kingdom had ever known, but by the time that he arrived at the English throne he was middle-aged and set in his ways, while the problems with which he was confronted were very different from those that he had so successfully faced in Edinburgh. All the same no vital concessions were wrung from the Crown during his reign, though on more than one occasion there was a definite clash with Parliament.

The accession of Charles I saw a rapid widening of the cleavage, and it would be a mistake to assume, as the Whig historians have done, that the right was all on one side, for it will hardly be denied that by this date Parliament represented the rich, who, as we have seen, made the laws at Westminster, and administered them on the bench in the country. They would have been more than human had they not looked to their own interests in these circumstances, and they proved to be very human indeed. James I had fully appreciated this, and when there had been rioting in the Midlands over enclosures he sent a Commission down to investigate, and warned the members to see that the poor were not impoverished by the encroachments of the rich. The House of Commons did not like this, nor did it like the great Prerogative Courts, such as the Star Chamber and the Council of the North, which stood between the rich and complete control of the machinery of justice. Yet a modern writer has said of the eleven years of the personal government of Charles I that they were characterized by "increasing efficiency in administration", and that "the interests of the wage-earning classes were never so carefully watched", while the disappearance of the Prerogative Courts "was much to be regretted".

The real weakness of Charles I lay in the fact that he was his own worst enemy, as a recent biographer has very well put it: "He was incapable of working up crowd emotion in his own favour. He could only state the issues as he saw them, not as they might appeal to the average man, which is the secret of successful propaganda". That the King had both precedent and commonsense on his side can hardly be denied, and his justification for the dissolution of Parliament in 1629 is a masterpiece of close reasoning. Had Charles been the innovator that hostile critics would have us believe, his methods would have been very different, and probably far more successful.

The weak position of the King was also in no small measure due to the fact that he united against him a growing body of opinion both in the Church and in the State. To some extent this was rather his misfortune than his fault. In the reign of Elizabeth, fear of the Spaniard had prevented any serious disunion among English Protestants, and in that of James I the country was too busy making money to think of much else. Before Charles had been long upon the throne both these factors had ceased to be operative, for the Continental Powers were too deeply implicated in the Thirty Years' War to have time for an invasion of the British Isles, while the squire, especially in the eastern counties, and the tradesman had reached that stage of affluence that gives leisure for an active interest in politics. It is unnecessary to discuss the question whether Laud's reforms and Strafford's policy were good in themselves, for, even if such were the case, it is clear that they were not practicable in the middle of the seventeenth century, when the current of public opinion in England and Scotland was running strongly in the opposite direction. The result of the King's dependence upon these two men created a feeling of suspicion, and it only required the attempt to enforce the liturgy in Scotland, and to levy Ship Money in England, to unloose a hurricane among the political classes. The former was a blunder which conclusively proves that Charles was badly advised upon Scottish matters, while the latter, though justifiable upon grounds of equity, was an excellent example of trying to do the right thing in the wrong way. In short, when the Long Parliament met, the King had hardly a friend in either House.

Fortunately for Charles, his very weakness at Westminster proved to be his strength in the country, for his opponents felt themselves so strong that they were tempted to go too far. They must, too, have believed that they were more secure than ever after the revealed incompetence of the Court in trying to arrest the Five Members in the House instead of rounding them up in their beds one dark night without any fuss. No politician regretted, for reasons which have been mentioned, the disappearance of the Courts of High Commission and Star Chamber, and very few murmured when the bishops were deprived of their seats in the House of Lords, but it was a very different matter when the majority in Parliament proceeded to wrest the control of the militia from the Crown, and, in return for Scottish help, set about presbyterianizing the Church of England. This provided Charles with a sufficient number of adherents to fight a civil war, and although he lost both it and his life, the monarchy was saved. The Restoration was in no small measure to be due to the disintegration of the forces that had over-thrown Charles I.

What is not always remembered is that the middle of the seventeenth century was a revolutionary era, for, as the late Jacques Bainville very truly wrote, *"ce 'grand siècle' n'est devenu celui de l'ordre qu'après avoir passé par le désorde"*. In Germany the Thirty Years' War had created a desert, while in France, Spain, and Italy there were disturbances which came within an ace of overturning the existing order. Such being the case it was hardly to be expected that Britain would escape the contagion, and, as it actually happened, the centrifugal forces gained a greater triumph there than anywhere else owing to the existence of certain conditions which were particularly favourable to them. It would, indeed, be a great mistake to ignore the international aspect of English revolutionary move-ments, and the Great Rebellion was to some extent but part of the general revolt against authority.

The Protectorate was the prototype of many a dictatorial regime of more recent times. It was a reaction against the licence of the sectaries, and an attempt to get back to all for which the old monarchy had stood on its material side, but without restoring the rightful monarch. At the same time Cromwell came a great deal nearer to ultimate victory than most of his later imitators, and had he lived longer, or had he left a reasonably competent elder son, and, above all, had he not pursued so fatal a foreign policy, the House of Cromwell might have established itself as the House of Hanover subsequently succeeded in doing. Even so, it could only have secured itself by doing what the Napoleons for a time managed to do, that is to say by obtaining the support of those who would normally have been the foremost defenders of the old dynasty. It would have been difficult for Oliver, who had played so prominent a part in the execution of Charles I, to have done this, but Richard might have been more successful.

As it was, the Protectorate represented but the rule of a faction that kept one man in power by brute force. Oliver realized this fact most clearly, and he did all that he could to get out of so difficult a position. He toyed with the idea of re-establishing the monarchy in his own person, and he attempted to draw up a constitution that should broaden the basis of his rule, just as Napoleon III was to do two hundred years later. It was all in vain, and in his short lifetime as Lord Protector there was a gulf between him and the mass of the English people which no constitutional compromise could bridge. The victories of his soldiers were the triumph, not of England but of his party, and the Royalists could fight for Spain against him without the great majority of their fellow-countrymen thinking any the worse of them for it. The historians of the nineteenth century did their best for Cromwell, but even they proved unable to convince their readers that he was a great national figure. Yet, as a statesman, there is this to be said for him; he was under no illusions as to the weakness of his hold upon the supreme power, and he never desired to rule merely in the name of a section.

The Restoration re-established the old conception of the monarchy as the one pre-eminently national institution. Masterly indeed was the skill with which Charles II enabled the Crown to play its old part of controlling the excesses of the parties in the interest of the nation, and when he prematurely died he had triumphed, amid the almost universal acclamation of his subjects, who knew that the King alone stood between them and anarchy. When he was recalled to the throne he had an empty treasury, no army, and a country that for twenty years had been a prey to every sort of disorder, material and intellectual. It was a prospect that might have appalled a superman, and it was not made any easier by the rapid degeneration of the House of Commons into one of the most corrupt legislative bodies known to history.

Charles II was the last King of England who not only actually governed the country, but was incomparably abler than any of his ministers. For twenty years he struggled to get things back to what they had once been: politician after politician attempted to thwart him, and catchword after catchword was invented to make wrong appear right. Yet the King never forgot that it was the party spirit carried to extremes that had brought his father to the scaffold, and he believed that the degradation of the Crown spelt the misery of the subject. It is true that throughout his reign the sabre-rattling of Cromwell's foreign policy was lacking, but then so was the distress which that foreign policy produced. By 1685 the country had recovered from the Civil War, and the power of the factions, which more than once since the Restoration had threatened to revive the old disturbances, had been broken, while their leaders were either in their graves or in exile. For the first time for nearly two generations the country was truly at peace.

It is surely one of the major tragedies of English

history that Charles II did not live for another twenty
years when he would have been succeeded, not by his
brother, but by his nephew. In three and a half
years James II undid the work of his predecessor,
and brought the traditional English monarchy crash-
ing to the ground. There can be no question of his
sincerity, but his precipitance defeated his own ends.
He rightly believed that the national interest required
the establishment of religious toleration, and that the
persecution of his Catholic co-religionists should
cease, but he went to work to secure this in such a way
as to give the impression that his object was to make
the Catholic minority dominant in the State: the
consequence was that the Church of England, which
had for all practical purposes elevated passive
obedience to a monarch reigning by divine right into
a dogma, was driven into opposition to the Crown.
James allowed himself to drift into the position of the
head of a party, and no very strong party at that,
with the natural consequence that when another,
and more powerful, party took the field against him
his position was desperate. Even so, he would in all
probability have prevailed had he attacked William
as soon as the Dutchman had landed, but James II
in 1688 was a very different man from the dashing
lieutenant of Turenne that he had been in his youth.

When James ascended the throne he had such an
opportunity as has been given to few monarchs. The
party which had brought his father to the scaffold,
and had given so much trouble to his brother, was
broken, and its leaders were in hopeless exile; Puritan-
ism was moribund, and the Church of England was
obsequious in its desire to carry out the wishes of the
Crown; and, above all, the King had not only a
standing army, but a full treasury which an almost
servile House of Commons hastened still further to

augment. As if these were not advantages enough, James had not been upon the throne more than a few months before he had crushed Monmouth's rebellion with consummate ease, and so proved to his enemies the hopelessness of resistance to his rule. Had James risen to the height of his opportunities he might have put the monarchy upon such a basis as to have preserved for ever that Balance of the Constitution which was to be upset to the great detriment of the national interest. Furthermore, he might have effected in Ireland, since he was of the race of one section of the people and of the religion of the other, a settlement which would have averted those unhappy disputes with England that have left such bitter memories in both countries. Unhappily, James did none of these things, but he acted in such a manner that within four years of succeeding to the Crown he was a fugitive on the soil of France.

That the Revolution of 1688 was the work of a minority is not denied by the Whigs themselves, and they were never under any illusion that they had the nation behind them. It is a common fallacy among historians and politicians to question the stability of this or that regime on the ground that it is but representative of a minority, for history contains innumerable examples of governments existing for generations on the support of a minority. Clemenceau even argued that every government is an oligarchy in the etymological sense, but without going so far as that it is impossible to deny that a government resting upon a minority may be, from its own point of view, highly successful, provided that its leaders realize the conditions upon which they are exercising power. The ruling oligarchy must see that enough people in key positions throughout the country are bound to it by ties of self-interest sufficiently strong to make

26

all attempt at resistance futile; that is to say these people will lose lucrative appointments, and quite probably their lives, if the oligarchy is overthrown. The Whigs grasped this thoroughly, and they acted accordingly.

So far as the monarchy was concerned, the immediate effect of the Revolution was to put the Crown back where it had been at the time of the Wars of the Roses, that is to say that it was reduced to the leadership of one of the factions in the State: it could no longer control the parties in the national interest. William III successfully revolted against such treatment on more than one occasion, and Anne made a decided attempt to follow her predecessor's example; as there was always a possibility that either of these sovereigns might come to some arrangement with the legitimate heir for his eventual succession, the Whigs refrained from pushing them too far. With the House of Hanover, however, the case was very different, and the dominant oligarchy did not hesitate to apply the screw, while the Fifteen strengthened its hand by demonstrating how unpopular the new dynasty really was. Indeed, the situation came to bear more than a superficial resemblance to that in the fifteenth century, for after 1715 it was quite clear that a change of the party in power would mean a change in the person of the monarch: so, as in the earlier period, the King was neither more nor less than a "good party man". That Venetian Constitution, which Disraeli the author so greatly derided but which Disraeli the statesman did so little to amend, thus came into existence in place of the old national monarchy that had stood above the parties and their strife.

There were protests against this conception of the Crown, and the most important of them was that voiced by Bolingbroke in his pamphlet. *The Idea of a*

Patriot King, which was published in 1749. It is to be noted that it was not until he had most signally failed as a statesman (where domestic affairs were concerned) that Bolingbroke began to acquire a reputation as a political philosopher; nevertheless in this book he showed a thorough grasp of the true principle of monarchy as the embodiment of the national idea. He wrote, of course, with the party purpose of providing Frederick, Prince of Wales, with a stick with which to belabour his father's ministers, but, with all his faults, Bolingbroke was too great a genius to produce an argument that should merely serve so transient an end. He stated the case for monarchy, and what he wrote holds for all time.

The weakness of Bolingbroke's thesis lay in the fact that it was impossible for any other than a legitimate dynasty to provide a Patriot King. The Hanoverians were regarded by a large part of the country as usurpers, and in the last resort they were dependent upon the minority whose fortunes were linked with theirs, for both in 1715 and in 1745 the English people had shown in no uncertain fashion that it was not prepared to lift a finger to keep them on the throne. In effect, those who thought with Bolingbroke wanted neither George II nor Frederick, Prince of Wales, but James III and VIII. Yet the power of the Crown under the Constitution was still very great, and it was no wonder that Bolingbroke did not see the flaw in his scheme. All the same, the Stuarts alone could have reigned as he wished the monarchs of England to reign, for their title in no way depended upon Parliamentary sanction.

It was not Frederick, but his son George III, who attempted to put into practice the theories of Bolingbroke, and in spite of the disability under which he suffered of not being the legitimate sovereign he succeeded to no inconsiderable extent. The decline of Jacobitism assisted him in a marked degree, since it regained for the ruling monarch the support of those who were naturally the bulwark of his throne, but who had been in opposition to it for two generations. Furthermore, the Whig oligarchy was becoming divided and enfeebled, and, after the collapse of the Elibank Plot in 1753 had shown that the danger from the Jacobites was at an end, the Whigs could no longer claim that they alone stood between England and a Popish Pretender. George III, too, if a man devoid of the higher gifts of statesmanship, knew exactly what he wanted, and this gave him a decided advantage over many of his opponents. He undoubtedly intended to be a Patriot King of the Bolingbroke type, and by the exercise of the royal authority to ensure that the quarrels of the factions were subordinated to the interests of the nation.

How far he might have gone towards the achievement of this goal in ordinary circumstances it is impossible to say, but the War of American Independence and his own health proved his undoing. Yet he never abandoned the attempt to enhance the power of the Crown, and so strong was this even after the disasters of the American war that the King was able to have his way about Catholic Emancipation in 1801, while six years later he scored an even more notable triumph, for he forced the ministry of "All the Talents" to resign, although it had a majority in the House of Commons. He then summoned the Duke of Portland to form an administration, and the result of the ensuing General Election showed that George had interpreted the wishes of his subjects correctly. In 1811, however, he became permanently insane, and in that year the reign of his son may be said to have begun.

It is not infrequently asserted that the decline of the power of the Crown commenced with the final relapse of George III into insanity, but this contention cannot in reality be maintained. George IV, both as Regent and King, entertained a very high opinion of his prerogative, which he was determined to do nothing to diminish, and the history of his relations with Canning in particular throws a good deal of light upon the position of the throne at that period. George disliked Canning personally, probably because of the statesman's espousal of the cause of Queen Caroline, and he disagreed with his policy, especially so far as the recognition of the revolted Spanish colonies in America were concerned. For years there was a struggle between the two men, but though George tried to hamper Canning at every turn, the Foreign Secretary never cast any doubt upon the King's right of interference; all he maintained was that it should be exercised in a constitutional manner, for George continually endeavoured to utilize his position as King of Hanover to oppose the official policy of his British ministers. So highly, indeed, did Canning think of the power of the Crown, in spite of his differences with the reigning monarch, that when he formed his ministry he endeavoured to enlist the throne in his support by reviving the post of Lord High Admiral for the Duke of Clarence.

That William IV did nothing to weaken the prerogative is proved by his action in 1834 when he dismissed a ministry that had a majority in the House of Commons, though his behaviour is not strictly comparable with that of his father in 1807, for he had the excuse of Lord Althorp's succession to a peerage, and the consequent necessity of finding a new Chancellor of the Exchequer.

Nevertheless, if the power of the monarch was

undiminished when William IV died the prestige of the monarchy itself had become very considerably dimmed, and it was freely predicted that Queen Victoria would be the last British soveriegn. If a monarch is to be the effective representative of the nation he must, in a civilized community, be himself the object of respect. George III had always retained his hold upon the affection of his subjects, and the fact that they respected him far more than they did most of his ministers had much to do with the success of his efforts to revive the power of the Crown. With his two successors it was otherwise. It is true that William was somewhat more estimable than his elder brother in his private life, but his whole outlook was that of a retired ship's captain. The throne had lost its dignity, and there was a reversion to the days of the first two Georges, without, however, the same necessity for the governing class to support the dynasty at all costs in case a worse thing befell.

In view of the rapid decline in the power of the Crown during the reign of Queen Victoria it will be well to see how matters stood when she came to the throne. The monarchy was, of course, purely a Parliamentary one, for George I and his descendants had only reigned by virtue of the Act of Settlement, for on the score of heredity alone there were many people who had a better claim than the new Queen. The King could not, indeed, govern against the wishes of the House of Commons, for the simple reason that if he did so he would soon find himself without the necessary funds to carry on the administration, and the royal veto had not been used since the House of Hanover came to the throne, but twice within a generation a ministry that had a majority in the Commons had been dismissed, while governments that wished to bring forward measures of which the monarch did not approve had been forced to resign, and all the lesser prerogatives, such as those of mercy, the making of treaties, the creation of peers, and the nomination to official appointments, were still intact.

Furthermore, since the Revolution the power of the Crown had not in any way been reduced by statute, and the various monarchs who had occupied the throne since that date had put very different constructions upon their rights under the Constitution. William III personally conducted the country's relations with its neighbours, and also commanded its armies in the field. Anne often attended the meetings of the Cabinet as well as the debates in the House of Lords, while she always claimed the right to appoint ministers according to her choice, and from any party. Of the Hanoverians, the first two had been content to allow the royal power, for the most part, to be exercised by the ruling oligarchy, but the last three had successfully prevented any usurpation of their prerogative. The position in 1837 thus was that a monarch who wished to exercise considerable personal influence upon the work of government would have found both the letter of the law, and a number of recent precedents, favourable to such a course.

Queen Victoria did not interpret her responsibilities in this way, with the not unnatural result that throughout her reign the power of the Crown was continually on the decline, as a careful perusal of the Queen's published letters clearly reveals. Sir Sidney Lee well summed up the position in the sentence, "Many times did she write to a minister that 'Never would she consent' to this or that proposal: yet her formal signature of approval was always at his service at the needful moment". Before long it began to be accepted that the non-participation of the Crown in the government of the country was a convention of the Constitution. Bagehot wrote in *The English Constitution* in 1872 that an English monarch "must sign his own death-warrant if the two Houses unanimously send it up to him", and Gladstone undoubtedly spoke for the Liberalism of his day when he wrote: "The ideas and practices of the time of George III, whose will in certain matters limited the action of the ministers, cannot be received otherwise than by what would be on their part nothing less than a base compliance or shameful subserviency dangerous to the public weal and in the highest degree disloyal to the dynasty. It would be an evil and a perilous day for the monarchy were any prospective posses or of the Crown to assume or claim for himself final or preponderating or even independent, power in any one department of the State".

The Conservative standpoint, at any rate after Disraeli had made his own opinions the official views of his party, was slightly different in theory, though almost identical in practice. It was the prestige, rather than the power, of the Crown which was increased when the Queen was made Empress of India, and Disraeli did nothing to arrest the decline of that power, while the Marquess of Salisbury was a pure Whig in these matters. If Queen Victoria had fewer differences of opinion with her Conservative than with her Liberal ministers, it was merely because she was generally in agreement with their policy, not because they allowed her more independence of action. The methods of her two greatest Premiers were different, for Gladstone addressed her as a public meeting, and Disraeli as a woman, but their attitude towards the Crown as an institution was much the same, though the Conservatives were certainly more attached to the Imperial idea than were their opponents.

During the Victorian era there was, nevertheless, no legislative diminution of the power of the Crown, which in theory was still considerable, as even Bagehot admitted: "It would very much surprise people if they were only told how many things the Queen could do without consulting Parliament, and it certainly has so proved, for when the Queen abolished purchase in the army by an act of pre-rogative (after the Lords had rejected the Bill for doing so), there was a great and general astonishment. But this is nothing to what the Queen can by law do without consulting Parliament. Not to mention other things, she could disband the army (by law she cannot engage more than a certain number of men, but she is not obliged to engage any men); she could dismiss all the officers, from the General Commanding-in-Chief downwards; she could dismiss all the sailors too; she could sell off all our ships of war and all our naval stores; she could make a peace by the sacrifice of Cornwall, and begin a war for the conquest of Brittany. She could make every citizen in the United Kingdom, male or female, a peer; she could make every parish in the United Kingdom a university; she could dismiss most of the civil servants; she could pardon all offenders. In a word, the Queen could by prerogative upset all the action of civil government within the government, could disgrace the nation by a bad war or peace, and could, by disbanding our forces, whether land or sea, leave us defenceless against foreign nations".

When the Queen died the great prerogatives of the Crown, therefore, were that of mercy, the dissolution and convocation of Parliament, the dismissal and selection of ministers, the declaration of war and peace, the making of treaties, the cession of territory, the creation of peers, and the nomination to official appointments. In addition, the monarch might refuse his assent to a Bill, but this right had not been exercised since the reign of Anne. On the other hand there must be taken into account the fact that Queen Victoria, owing to the accumulated experience of so many years, was able to exercise very considerable personal influence over her ministers; for in the latter part of her life she could quote from her own experience precedents relating to events that had occurred before some of them were even born, and this gave her an enormous advantage in her dealings with them. For example, when Campbell-Bannerman was Secretary of State for War he took some army scheme to the Queen for approval, and explained that it was an entirely new one. "No, Mr. Bannerman", was the reply, "Lord Palmerston proposed exactly the same thing to me in '52, and Lord Palmerston was wrong."

To no inconsiderable extent the diminution of the power of the Crown at this time was due to the withdrawal of the Queen from public life for many years after the death of the Prince Consort in 1861, and it is a curious commentary upon the character of the English people that this retirement on the part of the monarch should have been followed by the growth of a definite, if short-lived, republican movement. The English like to see their sovereigns, and the most popular have always been those who took obvious pleasure in showing themselves to their subjects. Charles II walking in St. James's Park, and feeding the ducks, where every Londoner who wished could watch him, is the model which the wise King of England will always keep before him. Such being the case it is hardly surprising that the long mourning in which Queen Victoria indulged for her dead husband, who had never been particularly popular in the land of his adoption, should have aroused a feeling of resentment, which was not lessened by the contemporaneous overthrow of monarchy in France.

Up to a certain point, indeed, the way for the republican movement had been paved by Thackeray, who lashed the House of Hanover with scorn in his lectures on *The Four Georges*, and who never lost an opportunity of ridiculing the stately ceremonial that had surrounded Louis XIV. This propaganda was not without its effect, and when the French Empire fell the working-classes, too, began to feel that the time had come for them to do something. On Sunday, September 19th, 1870, the Phrygian red cap was hoisted on poles in Trafalgar Square to the singing of the *Marseillaise*, and orators hailed the coming of the Republic of England. As a result of this demonstration a number of republican clubs were founded in London and the provinces, and Charles Bradlaugh, who had thrown himself wholeheartedly into the movement, published a pamphlet entitled *The Impeachment of the House of Brunswick.* It was couched in a peculiarly offensive style, and the author did not hesitate to attack altar as well as throne, for he compared the Trinity with a monkey with three tails. From his point of view this was a tactical blunder, for however little interest the English may take in the practice of religion, blasphemy of this nature is always repugnant to them.

In a short time Sir Charles Dilke (whose father had received a baronetcy for services to the Prince Consort), John Morley, and Joseph Chamberlain made their appearance upon the republican platform, and Chamberlain declared at a meeting in Birmingham, "I do not feel any great horror at the idea of the possible establishment of a republic in our country. I am quite certain that sooner or later it will come". John Richard Green, the historian, held the same views, and he went so far as to sneer at the Queen for her anxiety when the Prince of Wales was dangerously ill with typhoid fever. On March 19th, 1872, Dilke moved in the House of Commons for an enquiry into the Civil List, and he was supported by that most paradoxical of characters, Auberon Herbert, who in his youth had founded the Canning Club at Oxford. When the division was taken, the motion was rejected by 276 votes to 2, for its only supporters, in addition to the tellers, Dilke and Herbert, were Sir Wilfred Lawson, the temperance reformer, and George Anderson.

This outbreak of republicanism proved to be a mere flash in the pan. The upper and middle classes were, with the exceptions already quoted, solid in their support of the monarchy, and among the lower orders the overthrow of the throne only appealed to a few extremists, chiefly foreigners. Then there was the fact that a monarchical reaction set in before the republicans had time to get their campaign properly started, and they were never afterwards able to make any real headway. The nation had more heart than John Richard Green, and the recovery of the Prince of Wales awoke a widespread sympathy both for him and for his royal mother. Furthermore, the state of republican France, and of Spain, which was at the moment indulging in its favourite pastime of trying to exist without the Bourbons, was not such as to encourage Great Britain to conduct an experiment in republicanism. The Royal Family, too, had been by no means blind to the threat contained in the movement, and its members began once more to show themselves in public in the way that the people liked. As the years passed, and the Conservatives came into office, the Imperial conception of the Crown began to develop, and it was realized that the establishment of an English republic would spell the end of the British Empire. In these circumstances there were clearly no votes to be gained by a continued devotion to republicanism, and so, ere long, Dilke kissed hands upon appointment to a post in the ministry, while Morley finished his career as a peer of the realm; as for Chamberlain, he gave the Prince and Princess of Wales the warmest of greetings when they visited Birmingham, of which city he was then Mayor, and later still he was in 1897 the chief architect of that great monarchical demonstration, the Diamond Jubilee of Queen Victoria.

II

KING EDWARD VII

The Prince of Wales—Unfortunate Upbringing—Mistakes of Queen Victoria—The Court and Society—Popularity of the King—Relations with His Ministers—Further Decline of the Royal Power—The King's Interest in Foreign Affairs—International Situation on His Accession—Chamberlain and Germany—Kaiser Wilhelm II—British Relations with France—King Edward in Paris—His Triumph—Attitude towards Peter I of Serbia— Death of King Edward VII—The Financial Position of the Crown—Increasing Dependence on Parliament

KING EDWARD VII was born on November 9th, 1841, and he died on May 6th, 1910, but although over forty years have thus passed since his death it is not easy to pass a final judgment upon his career because of lack of documentation. His letters, without which the relevant evidence cannot be considered complete, have not, save for a limited selection edited some years ago by Lieut.-Colonel J. P. C. Sewell, been given to the world by his successors on the throne, although, as it is not without interest to note, those of his mother began to make their appearance only six years after her death.

As Prince of Wales he has been compared with Shakespeare's Prince Hal, who became the model monarch King Henry V, and there is something in the comparison, though it must be remembered that even in his feverish youth he never allowed his pleasures to interfere with the performance of his duties. What, too, is often forgotten in this connection is that no Prince of Wales ever had to serve so long an apprenticeship to monarchy as he did, for at the time of his accession he was in his sixtieth year. His education had been of the most deplorable and unsuitable kind, under the well-intentioned, but wholly misguided, direction of the Prince Consort and Baron Stockmar. Queen Victoria not only inherited that attitude of suspicion towards the Heir Apparent which marked all the rulers of the House of Hanover, but, with the passage of time and under the influence of her husband, she became obsessed with the fear that her eldest son might come to resemble her uncles in general, and the so-called First Gentleman of Europe in particular. Unhappily, in her attempt to prevent such a development she adopted, like so many parents in every walk of life, the very methods most calculated to produce the result she was at such pains to avoid.

When the Prince came of age, shortly after his father's early death, the Queen refused to allow him to have any regular and responsible employment, so that he was compelled to expend his enormous energies, and to dissipate his great and growing powers, on a number of petty, and in some cases unworthy, pursuits. Such, rather than any real tendency to vice, was the explanation of the Tranby Croft scandal and of the Prince's appearance in the Mordaunt case. Yet he travelled widely, both abroad and in what was then the British Empire, he took the lead in many notable philanthropic movements, especially those which had as their object the provision of houses and hospitals for the poorer classes; and he did a great deal to raise the tone of sport. From politics, however, he was excluded. In vain one Premier after another, Conservative and Liberal alike, implored the Queen to give him some work to do, whether it was to learn the routine of government departments, to go through the discipline of the Army, to administer India, or, above all, to live in Ireland as his mother's representative. The Queen was adamant in her refusal, "evidently haunted", to quote the late Professor Hearnshaw, "by the fear that Albert Edward if allowed any independence would develop the undesirable filial features of one or other of the four Georges". Queen Victoria may or may not have been a great monarch, but she was a poor mother to her eldest son. In the circumstances the astonishing thing is not that her heir kicked over the traces so much but that he did it so little.

Both as Prince and King he touched life at many points, and that was not the least of the reasons for his success. Society in the Victorian era despised what it called "trade", though such an attitude was some- what illogical on the part of the children and grand- children of "nabobs" and of the profiteers of the Revolutionary and Napoleonic Wars. There was, too, an exclusiveness about the Court which was largely due to the German origin of the dynasty, but which was also to some extent the result of the unpopularity of the earlier Georges. Queen Victoria's outlook in these matters was influenced by that of the Prince Consort, and this was typically Teutonic. On occasion this rigidity could have humorous, if un- intended, consequences. At the Drawing Rooms, for example, the Queen was in the habit of kissing the daughters of dukes, marquesses, and earls, who were being presented for the first time. At one such cere- mony Her Majesty, quite inadvertently, was about to salute the wife of a knight in this way, when a Gentle- man-in-Waiting audibly whispered, "Don't kiss her, Your Majesty, she's not a real lady". Her father, the Duke of Kent, was a martinet, and his daughter seems to have inherited his characteristics in this respect.

The Queen would never have sat down to dinner with a playwright, as Louis XIV had done with Molière and Racine, but her oldest son revived, to the great advantage of the Royal Family, the older and more generous traditions of the monarchy. Both before and after he ascended the throne he delighted to honour any who showed themselves worthy, whatever their origin, and he brought royalty into personal contact with far wider sections of the population than had been the case since the fall of the Stuarts.

There might be one or two people at Marlborough House or Buckingham Palace who need not have been received there, and the standard of aristocratic behaviour may have fallen somewhat in the opening years of the twentieth century, but the country as a whole rejoiced in the revival of the old pageantry of the monarchy which followed the death of Queen Victoria. The importance of this aspect of the King's activities can hardly be over-rated, and so the man-in-the-street, who had respected the old Queen, came to love "Teddy" as his ancestors had loved "Old Rowley". During the darker days of the First World War it was no rare thing to hear the remark, "This wouldn't have happened if Teddy had been alive"— an observation which, whether true or not, testified to the affection in which King Edward VII was held by his subjects. Nobody would have described him as an erudite, or even as a moderately well-read, man, but he kept in touch with many distinguished artists and men of letters through such personal friends as Lord Leighton.

The remarkable thing about the King's attitude was that this broadening of the basis of the throne was effected without any cheapening of royalty. King Edward was no Louis Philippe. No one was more particular in matters of etiquette or dress than he, and there are many anecdotes of the quickness with which he would notice the least departure from propriety in either. Yet with the mass of the people he was more popular than any monarch since Charles II, and it was largely because he shared in the amusements of a sport-loving nation. Illogical as it may appear to the philosopher, his three successes in the Derby forged a link between him and his fellow-countrymen which meant more than all the provisions of the Constitution. Moreover, except perhaps during the last two years of his life, when a profound melancholy was creeping over him, he always looked cheerful in public, and this goes a long way with the man-in-the-street. In short, it is not too much to say that the work of King Edward VII in this sphere was of the utmost assistance to his successors in a revolutionary age when every institution, divine and human, was called in question.

Of King Edward's relations with his ministers, and of his influence upon the working of the Constitution, it will not be possible to speak with any confidence until his letters have been published in full. He was not very interested in domestic politics, except in their broader aspects, and, like his successor, he had little patience with anything which in his opinion savoured too much of the "parish pump". Whenever possible he did his best to soften the asperities of of party strife. For example, when the Conservative Government resigned in December, 1905, he asked Mr. Walter Long, the retiring Chief Secretary for Ireland, to get into touch with Mr. Bryce, who was to succeed him, and, to quote Mr. Long, "tell him quite frankly and freely what are your views of the difficulties connected with the Government of Ireland apart from the question of Home Rule; what you believe to be the most essential details of administration; and, in other words, give him the benefit of your knowledge and experience just as you would if you were being followed by some political friend of your own".

During King Edward's reign there were four Prime Ministers, namely Lord Salisbury, Mr. Balfour, Sir Henry Campbell-Bannerman, and Mr. Asquith. The first of these resigned office before the King had been long upon the throne, and during the period of his Premiership the pre-occupation of the Government was the termination of the South African War. With Lord Salisbury's successor the King was never on very easy terms, and there was a marked contrast in the temperaments of the two men. King Edward was a man of the world in the best sense of that much-abused term, while about Mr. Balfour there was, it must be confessed, a good deal of the intellectual snob. The King, in his idle moments, read French novels, while the Prime Minister, on similar occasions, perused volumes of German philosophy, so it is hardly surprising that monarch and Premier should have had widely different outlooks. King Edward also distrusted Mr. Balfour's private secretary, J. S. Sanders, whose influence over his chief was considerable, and there was a strong Whig element in the Government, Conservative though it nominally was, which was hardly likely to see eye to eye with the sovereign in constitutional matters.

With his two Liberal Prime Ministers, on the other hand, and particularly with Sir Henry Campbell-Bannerman, King Edward's relations were a great deal more cordial, and this lent colour to the popular belief among Conservatives at the time that the monarch was a Radical and a Home Ruler. The Liberals were also more tactful in their dealings with the King, and although he was sometimes irritated by the outbursts of Mr. Lloyd George he was able to work with Sir Henry and Mr. Asquith in a more friendly spirit than with the previous administration; in particular, he did a great deal to ensure the success of the Haldane Army reforms and of Fisher's reconstruction of the Navy. What would have happened had he lived a few years longer, and been confronted with the House of Lords and Ulster crises in their full force, it is impossible to say, but his wisdom and tact might have removed some of the bitterness which marked party politics in the period immediately preceding the First World War. With Joseph Chamberlain, the bugbear of his mother in her earlier days, the King's relations were always cordial, and there was an additional bond between the two men in the fact that their elder sons had been friends at Cambridge.

The success of King Edward VII in reviving the old pageantry that was associated with the monarchy in the past cannot, however, conceal the fact that during his reign the Crown steadily lost ground from the constitutional standpoint. While he was on the throne most of the great prerogatives were challenged, and in each case the King was forced to give way: in this connection, too, it is not without interest to note that these limitations of the prerogative were mainly due to the efforts of the Conservatives. For example, when a cession of territory was necessary as a result of the conclusion of the Franco-British Entente in 1904, Mr. Balfour took the view that the consent of Parliament was essential, while he also advanced the opinion not only that the House of Commons could insist upon a dissolution but also that ministers might be selected or dismissed by the Premier without reference to the Crown.

The exact working of the Constitution under King Edward VII is just one of those points upon which the necessary information will not be available until his correspondence is published, but it would appear that the monarch himself only made two serious political mistakes, given the circumstances in which the monarchy had been reduced to doing its work. They were both in that year 1908, when his judgment was not what it had been: in April, when Sir Henry Campbell-Bannerman resigned, instead of returning home to superintend the reconstruction of the Cabinet, he summoned Mr. Asquith to Biarritz, and in the following July he refrained from inviting to a garden party at Windsor certain M.P.s who had adversely criticized his recent visit to the Tsar. In the latter case he eventually gave way, and the invitations were sent, but the King decided not to hold any more garden parties at which he was not permitted to select his guests.

There is also considerable reason to believe that when the Liberal administration was being formed after the resignation of Mr. Balfour in December, 1905, the King made every effort to induce Campbell-Bannerman to include Sir Charles Dilke in his administration as Foreign Secretary, and that he only desisted when the new Prime Minister declared that if King Edward continued to insist he would have to find another Premier. The monarch was also a strong supporter of the Deceased Wife's Sister Marriage Bill, which became law in 1908. The measure was disliked by certain elements in the Church of England, and to overcome their opposition in the House of Lords the King let it be known that he wished to see the Bill passed. These would appear to be the only two instances where King Edward actively intervened in domestic political matters.

It is not, however, round his attitude towards home

politics that controversy has raged most fiercely but rather in respect of the line he adopted in foreign affairs, a subject in which he was keenly interested and upon which he held decided views. In this matter there are two schools of thought. In Germany he was regarded as little better than a fiend in human guise, and Princess Blücher could write from Berlin after his death: "Popular hatred here is centred on the shade of King Edward VII; he is supposed to have been the moving spirit in forming the encirclement of Germany". In the Reichstag in August, 1915, the Imperial Chancellor, Herr von Bethmann-Hollweg, declared: "King Edward VII believed that his principal task was to isolate Germany. The encirclement by the Entente with openly hostile tendencies was drawn closer year by year. We were compelled to reply to this situation with the Greatest Armament Budget of 1913". On the other hand there are those who maintain that even in the formation of the Anglo-French Entente the King played no great part, and that the foreign policy of the reign was in reality wholly conducted by the two Foreign Secretaries, the Marquess of Lansdowne and Sir Edward Grey. The point is no mere academic one, because it concerns British relations with Germany at a critical period of European history, and their record contains more than one lesson for a later generation.

During the long period when he was Prince of Wales there were three influences which much affected the future King's attitude towards international affairs. First of all, there was in his extreme youth the Crimean War, and the close relations which for a time existed between the British Royal Family and Napoleon III; these had the effect of making him intensely pro-French and anti-Russian. Then there was his marriage to Princess Alexandra of Denmark, which was so

soon followed by a German attack upon his wife's
country; from that date the Prince was pronouncedly
pro-Danish and anti-Prussian. Lastly there occurred
the long Premiership of Palmerston during his most
impressionable years: this, in its turn, fixed in him a
permanent leaning towards an active foreign policy.
As the nineteenth century drew to its close there was
also the growth of personal antipathy between him and
his nephew, Kaiser Wilhelm II. The consequences
of this last circumstance have often been exaggerated,
but it is impossible to resist the conclusion that the
suspicion and dislike with which King Edward was
regarded by the Kaiser had some influence upon
German policy, and that this in its turn further
estranged uncle and nephew until the vicious circle
was complete.

Queen Victoria had no more allowed her eldest son
to play a part in foreign than in home politics, and
although she had herself exercised a fairly strong
negative influence over the monarchs of the Continent
she exercised it from home. She travelled but little,
and when she went abroad it was as a private person.
Only once during her sixty-three years' reign did she
pay an official visit to a foreign country, and that was
in 1855, when, with the Prince Consort, she went to
Paris. The Prince of Wales acted very differently. He
loved the Continent; he liked meeting his foreign
relatives and their ministers; he revelled in ceremonial;
and he was at his best in the midst of the magnificent
pageantry which still characterized the Courts of
Europe. In addition, the Prince was a first-rate
linguist, and a true cosmopolitan who felt himself at
home anywhere. He early acquired a clear knowledge
of international affairs, together with a shrewd idea
where British interests lay; while he managed, without
ceasing to be a "good European", to advance the

cause of his own country. In spite of the obstacles placed in his path by his mother King Edward VII was, at the time of his accession, remarkably well qualified to collaborate with his ministers in the field of international affairs.

The position of Great Britain in 1901 was not what it had been. Lord Salisbury had for many years combined the offices of Prime Minister and Foreign Secretary, but, in the opinion of one of his successors in the second capacity, he was, by the turn of the century, "weakly temporising and without initiative to meet the new conditions of a rapidly changing world". He was still Prime Minister, but had recently been succeeded at the Foreign Office by the Marquess of Lansdowne. The policy of splendid isolation which had been pursued for several decades had, as was proved when disasters came thick during the early weeks of the South African War, left Britain without a friend in Europe, and only her overwhelming naval supremacy had prevented the formation of a coalition against her at that time. With France relations were hardly less strained than they had been during the Fashoda incident, and memories were still fresh of the contest between Joseph Chamberlain and Hanotaux. Russia was feared and her intentions suspected, as had been the case during the greater part of the nineteenth century. Germany, with whom Britain had hitherto been on the best of terms, was showing signs of becoming unfriendly, and the Kaiser's telegram to President Kruger on the morrow of the Jameson Raid had been by no means wholly forgotten. The situation, in short, was far from reassuring.

So much was common ground, but there were differences of opinion as to the remedies to be applied. For some years Joseph Chamberlain, then Colonial Secretary and the foremost member of the Salisbury administration, had been advocating a foreign policy based on the closest collaboration with Germany and the United States, and he had been given a remarkably free hand by the Cabinet to put his ideas into practice, though the old Prime Minister himself was more than a little sceptical about his colleague's chances of success. The first advances of the Colonial Secretary, made in 1898 and the succeeding year, were not well received in Berlin, where they were regarded as proof of British weakness, and Chamberlain sustained a severe rebuff at the hands of the Imperial Chancellor, Prince von Bülow, which caused him to remark to the Kaiser that the German statesman was "a bad man to go tiger-shooting with".

In spite of this setback the Cabinet agreed to allow their colleague to try again, so when the Boer armies were in flight, and the General Election of 1900 had returned the Government to power with an unimpaired majority, the Colonial Secretary once more got in touch with Baron von Eckardstein, his friend and intermediary in all negotiations with the Wilhelmstrasse. In the very month that King Edward came to the throne Chamberlain told Eckardstein that the moment had come for Great Britain to abandon her policy of isolation, and to link herself either with the Triple Alliance of Germany, Austria-Hungary, and Italy, or with Russia and France. In this connection it must be remembered that the revelation of Russian military weakness in the war against Japan still lay ahead, and that these two combinations of Powers were generally regarded as constituting a balance. Chamberlain said that he would himself prefer closer relations with Germany, and that in his opinion a beginning could best be made by a secret agreement concerning Morocco. If the German Government refused, Great Britain would be obliged to make a treaty with Russia, even at the price of considerable sacrifices in China and on the Persian Gulf.

Accordingly negotiations were resumed, and they dragged on for some six months, though, warned by his previous experience, the Colonial Secretary left the principal part in the conduct of them to Lord Lansdowne. That they came to nothing was largely due to that evil genius of the Hohenzollern Reich, namely Baron von Holstein, who kept instilling into the Kaiser and the Imperial Chancellor the belief that Great Britain had always pursued the policy of getting others to pick her chestnuts out of the fire, and that this was why she wanted an agreement with Germany. He did not believe that there was any possibility of an understanding between London and Paris, and therefore Germany was in a position to sell her friendship at a very high price.

Far from opposing this move on the part of his ministers King Edward did everything that he could to second it. In August, 1901, he had a long interview with the Kaiser at Wilhelmshöhe; but the meeting proved a failure, for it left both upon King and the British Government the impression that, to quote Sir Sidney Lee, "the Kaiser was insincere in his protestations for an alliance, and that the chauvinist tone of the German press more correctly represented the attitude of Germany". Meanwhile Chamberlain was becoming increasingly restive, though Prince von Bülow remained deaf to warnings that the Colonial Secretary's attitude was changing. In the summer *The Times* openly advocated an understanding with Russia, and called attention to the growing strength of the German Navy. As the months passed an Anglo-German alliance was seen to be a mere dream, and the winter witnessed an exchange of polemics between Chamberlain and the Imperial Chancellor which marked the end of the attempt to arrive at an understanding with Berlin.

Joseph Chamberlain had now learned the lesson which was one day in even more tragic circumstances to be forced upon his younger son, namely the impossibility of coming to an understanding with Germany. Every concession was either regarded as weakness or was used as an excuse for making another demand. King Edward had probably reached this conclusion earlier, but, if so, it made no difference to his efforts to further his Government's policy of friendship with Berlin. This arch-conspirator of encirclement left no stone unturned to come to an agreement with Germany, and when the Anglo-Japanese Alliance was concluded at the end of January, 1902, he insisted that the German Government should be informed at once. So much for the legend that King Edward VII was always working against the Reich. On the contrary, the Franco-British Entente would never have been formed, and Great Britain would have become the ally of Germany, had it not been for the attitude of the Kaiser, the Imperial Chancellor, and, above all, Baron von Holstein.

It would be untrue to say that King Edward initiated, or even played the leading part in, the negotiations with France which then took place, but it is extremely doubtful whether they would have been successful without him. He created the atmosphere in which the statesmen of the two countries were able to collaborate. The turning-point was his visit to Paris in May, 1903. As Prince of Wales in the days of his youth he had been a favourite in the French capital, but since then Great Britain and France had more than once been on the verge of war, while French sympathy for the Boers was notorious. The visit to Paris was therefore one of the most critical episodes of the King's life, and as he drove down the Champs Elysées, on his way from the Bois de Boulogne station, the crowd was sullenly respectful, and few were the hats that were doffed; here and there, too, were heard cries of *"Vivent les Boers"*, *"Vive Marchand"*, and *"Vive Fashoda"*. "The French don't like us", somebody remarked to the King. "Why should they?" was the characteristic reply, and before the visit was over the scene was completely changed.

King Edward neglected no opportunity of impressing upon the French his desire to be their friend, and one incident will suffice to illustrate the scrupulous attention which he paid to detail. One evening, accompanied by his suite, he went to the Théâtre Français. The house was full, but the public were icy, so during the interval the King left his box with the intention of winning this hostile crowd to his side. In the lobby he saw an actress whom he had met in London. Holding out his hand, he said, "Oh, Mademoiselle, I remember how I applauded you in London. You personified there all the grace, all the *esprit* of France". Never had King Edward better displayed his ability to say and do the right thing: the remark spread like wildfire, and the ice was broken. The incident, moreover, was typical. In the streets and at official receptions, in public and in private, he exerted all his tremendous powers of charm, with the result that when he left Paris the route was lined with a madly enthusiastic crowd, and where there had been cries of *"Vivent les Boers"* there were now shouts of *"Vive notre Roi"*. This visit should surely be classed among the greatest personal triumphs in recent history.

During the months which elapsed before the Entente was concluded King Edward gave invaluable support to his ministers. The policy they were pursuing was more to his liking, it is true, than that of an agreement with Germany, but he never forgot his *rôle* under the Constitution as it had come to be worked, and he did as much to further the Government's efforts in the one case as in the other. The King's part in the conclusion of the Franco-British Entente was later well defined by Poincaré, when he said, "Not one of my fellow-countrymen has forgotten the happy impetus given on that decisive occasion by His Majesty King Edward VII to the work of concord which has outlived him".

When, in due course, the time came to include Russia in the Entente the King once more did everything in his power to help the Government of the day, and it was an indirect consequence of these efforts that, as already mentioned, he fell foul of certain Radicals and Socialists who objected to any understanding with Russia on what a later generation would have described as ideological grounds. During international friction at the time of the separation of Norway from Sweden, and again when difficulties arose between Turkey and Greece over the question of Crete, his good offices did much to lead to a peaceful settlement. Either or both of these crises might have led to war had they not been properly handled, and it was by his attitude on these and similar occasions that King Edward earned his title of the Peacemaker.

He had, of course, the advantage of living in an age when British statesmen still honoured the monarchical principle in theory, however much they might desire to circumscribe the power of any particular monarch in practice. In 1889, for example, the British Government refused to participate in the Paris Exhibition of that year on the ground that its primary object was to commemorate the centenary of the French Revolution, an event of which Great Britain, as a monarchical

Power, could not approve. Then, again, it was not until three years after the murder of King Alexander I of Serbia that Great Britain resumed diplomatic relations with that country.

The attitude of King Edward on this last occasion is illustrative of his conception of his position. When he was told that Austria-Hungary and Russia were prepared to recognize the new Serbian regime, he observed that they were interested countries, and there was "no need for England to recognize a government consisting of assassins". The new Serbian monarch, King Peter I, was, however, very desirous of recognition, and he induced the Tsar and King Victor Emmanuel III of Italy to instruct their ambassadors to take the matter up with King Edward personally. He received them in audience at Windsor and gave a reply which must be quoted in full: "I regret very much indeed that I cannot comply with your suggestions. The assassination of King Alexander and Queen Draga was so terrible that it made a deep impression on public opinion in England. Public opinion has not yet recovered from the shock, and would certainly not approve of a re-establishment of diplomatic relations with Serbia; and you know well that I and my government must take into account the public opinion of our country. And, besides this reason, I have another, and, so to say, a personal reason. *Mon métier à moi est d'être Roi.* King Alexander was also by his *métier un Roi.* As you see, we belonged to the same guild, as labourers or professional men. I cannot be indifferent to the assassination of a member of my profession, or, if you like, a member of my guild. We should be obliged to shut up our businesses if we, the Kings, were to consider the assassination of Kings as of no consequence at all. I regret, but you see that I cannot do what you wish me to do". It was not until the principal regicides had been placed upon the retired list that recognition was granted.

It has already been seen how the development of the Imperial idea enhanced the prestige, though not the power, of the Crown during the reign of Queen Victoria, and no account, however brief, of King Edward's life and work would be complete without some reference to his interest in the Empire overseas and in the United States.

In his youth he had travelled in all parts of the world, and he was the only English monarch since his namesake, Edward I, to set foot in the East. When he came to the throne he sent the Prince of Wales to represent him at the opening of the first Commonwealth Parliament in Australia, and his reception of the Boer generals at the close of the South African War did much to create the atmosphere which rendered possible the establishment of the Union of South Africa. It was a matter of the deepest regret to him that he was unable to visit Canada for the tercentenary celebrations of the founding of Quebec in 1908, but that particular year was a critical one in Europe, and it behoved the King to remain, if not at home, at any rate within easy reach of home. Towards Ireland he was always sympathetic, and his feelings were cordially reciprocated by his Irish subjects; indeed, had his ministers shared his insight where Ireland was concerned the history of the United Kingdom might have been very different. With regard to India it was the same: his tour of that country in 1875-76 had given him a keen perception of its administration and of the personalities of the native princes, and this interest he retained until his death. As for the United States, which the King had visited as Prince of Wales, he was on the friendliest terms with many Americans of both sexes, while Mr. Whitelaw

Reid was one of his intimates. President Theodore Roosevelt he never saw, but the correspondence between the two men is eloquent of the cordial relations which existed where they were concerned, and the King gave evidence of his feelings towards the United States in his prediction that if Mr. Roosevelt would visit England he would "see what a reception would be given to the President of the United States by the King of Great Britain and Ireland and by his people."

With the coming of the year 1908 the shadows began to lengthen, and it became clear that the King's health was breaking down. He had long been troubled with attacks of bronchitis, and now his heart began to be seriously affected. He became subject to despondency and melancholy, and, ignoring the results of his own life's work, in one of these fits of depression he made the gloomy prophecy, "My son may reign, but my grandson never will." At home the situation was becoming tense with the rejection of the Budget by the House of Lords and with increasing social unrest, while abroad the King never forgave the Emperor Francis Joseph for the deception which he considered had been practised upon him in the matter of the Austrian annexation of Bosnia and Herzegovina. In fact the reign closed amid the gathering clouds that heralded a storm of which the violence is still very far from spent. It was the end of an era both for Britain and for the world.

Among the many tributes to the statesmanship of King Edward VII which might be quoted, two are specially valuable. The first comes from Sir William Harcourt, a Radical and a man of very independent character, who said "this was the greatest man that ever I had speech with". The second was that of Lord Esher, from whom little was hidden concerning monarchs and their ways: "The King is dead. . . .

Towards politicians, even towards those who worried him, I never knew him to be unjust. . . . He had an instinct for statecraft which carried him straight to the core of a great problem without deep or profound knowledge of the subject. He had one supreme gift, and this was his unerring judgment of men and women".

Before, however, passing to a consideration of the crisis in the midst of which King George V ascended the throne, it will not be out of place to turn to the finances of the Royal Family, since at the accession of King Edward VII a commission was appointed to examine them. To this body Sir Francis Knollys was able to announce, "It is my happy duty to inform you that, for the first time in English history, the heir-apparent comes forward to claim his right to the throne unencumbered by a single penny of debt". It was a welcome change from the days of the First Gentleman of Europe who owed no less than £260,000 at the age of twenty-four.

There is a widespread belief that the Civil List represents the annual allowance which a generous nation makes to its Royal Family. In reality this amounts to about half the sum which the State receives from the Crown as a result of the surrender of the revenues from its landed property which is now made at the beginning of each reign; so that far from being, as is sometimes alleged, unduly lavish, the nation actually makes a handsome profit on the transaction.

Before the Revolution of 1688 the King had the disposal of all revenue, and the duty of the Treasury officials was the pay it out as the monarch directed. It was no concern of theirs whether it went to some royal mistress or favourite, or to pay for the upkeep of the Navy. The money came from many sources, such as subsidies voted by Parliament, Customs receipts, and the Crown lands, but it was, so to speak, all paid into one account: there was no separate fund for the Royal Family. Incidentally, this explains why the House of Commons always objected so strongly to the alienation of the Crown lands to the sovereign's friends, because the less the King obtained by way of revenue from that source, the more he was sure to demand from Parliament, for he had to meet all the expenses of the State. For many centuries the established theory was that at any rate in normal circumstances, the King should "live of his own".

With the accession of William and Mary a change was made, and a definite Civil List was created: it was so called because it was meant to defray the whole charge of civil expenditure. Defence was excluded, for with the attempt of James II to create a standing army still fresh in their minds, the triumphant Whigs had no intention of giving the Crown a free hand with the Navy and Army. In 1689, then, £600,000 was appropriated out of the entire national revenue, including the hereditary revenues of the Crown, for the Civil List. Out of this William III had to pay the cost of the royal household, palaces, and gardens, as well as the salaries of the Diplomatic Service, the Civil Service, and the judges, together with all pensions granted by him or his predecessors.

The system continued under Anne and George I, though the amount received by the Crown under this head varied. With George II a new arrangement was made. Parliament guaranteed him an income of £800,000 a year if the hereditary revenues, together with those provided by Parliament, fell short of that sum; but the King was to take the benefit of any surplus which might accrue. George III slightly varied this arrangement, for in return for the same income which his grandfather had received he surrendered his rights to most of the revenues from the Crown lands, the Excise, and the Post Office. The Court of "Farmer George" was frugal to a degree, but the King himself was always in financial difficulties, though it must be admitted that this was to no small extent due to the amount he spent on bribing members of Parliament. After the loss of the American colonies in 1783 the country was on the verge of bankruptcy, and the reform of the Civil List was taken in hand. It was divided into categories, which commenced with the Royal Family, and these were to be paid in a prescribed order: last on the list came the Chancellor of the Exchequer and the Treasury officials, the idea being to stimulate them by this means into greater activity, since unless there was vigilance over income and economy in expenditure, they would not get paid at all.

The early years of the nineteenth century witnessed further changes, necessitated by the increasing complexity of internal administration. In 1816 various payments to members of the Royal Family were transferred from the Civil List to the Consolidated Fund, and George IV surrendered to Parliament all the hereditary revenues of England and Ireland, while his successor gave up those of Ireland in addition. In return, the Civil List of William IV was relieved of all public charges except £23,000 for Secret Service money. This practice was soon carried further, and the pay of public servants was wholly removed from the Civil List, and henceforth appeared on the votes, or was charged on the Consolidated Fund. In these circumstances the term Civil List pensions became an anarchronism, for they, too, were paid out of the Consolidated Fund. On the other hand, the King continued to enjoy the revenues of the Duchy of Lancaster, while the Prince of Wales (when there is one) is supported by those of the Duchy of Cornwall. Owing to different methods of accounting it is not easy to compare the income of British monarchs with that of their foreign contemporaries, but at the accession of King Edward VII it was officially stated that his Privy Purse was very much less than that of the Austrian, Russian, and German Emperors, or of the Kings of Italy and Spain.

In conclusion it may be added that the King is free of taxation in respect of income and property coming to him in right of the Crown, that is to say the Civil List, but his private estates, and any income he may derive from private investments, are subject to the ordinary rates and taxes which his subjects have to pay. He does enjoy one or two minor privileges: his telegrams have precedence and go free, and his letters are franked in the post. He does not pay probate or death duty on legacies left to him, or on property he inherits, nor is his will lodged at Somerset House. When the Income Tax was revived in 1842 Queen Victoria agreed to pay it voluntarily, as it was generally considered a monstrous imposition, and she wished to set the country a good example. Payment was continued by King Edward VII, but in the arrangement of the Civil List at the accession of his son it was discontinued. Finally, the King does not pay rates in respect of his palaces, since they are State buildings, and as such are exempt from local charges.

It is not a little significant that the achievement by Parliament of almost complete financial control over the Crown should have coincided with the steady decline of the political power of the monarchy.

KING GEORGE V

Iᴛ ʜᴀs already been pointed out that at the time of the death of King Edward VII a serious political and constitutional crisis was in process of development, and during the first four years of the reign of his successor the impact of events at Westminster upon the Crown was very considerable. Britain was passing once more into a revolutionary age, and in these circumstances the throne could not expect to remain unaffected.

The beginning of this movement was the General Election of 1906 which returned the Liberals to power with a record majority. "The recent elections", Sir Wilfrid Laurier, then Prime Minister of Canada, wrote to Professor Hewins "have undoubtedly opened a new era in the history of England. The England of the past may survive partially yet for a few years, but it is a democratic England which now takes its place. The Labour element will count henceforth as a very important factor, and it is difficult to foresee exactly to what extent, but certainly to a very large extent, it will control legislation". History has shown that there was much truth in this observation, and although the turning-points in the life of nations are not so clearly defined as some authorities would have us believe, it is difficult in the light of more recent events to resist the conclusion that 1906 represents a very definite landmark in the national annals. In that year the nineteenth century really ended, though its ghost was to walk until 1914; social and economic, rather than political, problems became the more important; while abroad the *status quo*, which had existed relatively intact for nearly a century, began to give evidence of its approaching collapse. The writing was on the wall, even if it was noticed by comparatively few.

Nevertheless, it is doubtful if, in the opening weeks of 1906, anyone would have given credence to a prophecy of what actually was to take place before the then Prince of Wales was in his grave. Who, for instance, on the morrow of the greatest victory that the Liberal party had ever known, would have believed that it was the last triumph that party was to enjoy? Or that in less than a generation it would be reduced to a mere handful? Yet this was but a further stage in a process that had already begun. When, in 1886, Liberalism lost its Right Wing the party was necessarily driven to the Left, but the rise of the Labour party deprived it of the very backing upon which it had now become dependent. Furthermore, the political problems which had for long supplied its *raison d'être* were solved, or were in process of solution, and with economic and social questions it was to prove, somewhat unexpectedly, quite ill-fitted to deal.

The General Election had taken place in January, 1906, but the municipal contests in the following November showed that the Liberal tide was already on the ebb, while in March, 1907, an event took place of which the significance could not fail to be observed. The London County Council had for a considerable period been under Progressive control, but the Municipal Reformers now won a crushing victory by the net gain of no less than forty-four seats. The year 1908 witnessed a long series of Government defeats at by-elections, and the most notable of these Conservative successes was at North-West Manchester, where Mr. Joynson-Hicks defeated Mr. Winston Churchill, who was seeking re-election on his appointment as President of the Board of Trade, as was necessary under the existing law.

To no inconsiderable extent these reverses indicated the natural swing of the pendulum after the triumph of the General Election, but there was more to them than that. The Government's legislative record had not been brilliant, and it had dissatisfied some sections of opinion while alarming others. The Old Age Pensions Act, though originally a proposal of Joseph Chamberlain, was certainly an item on the asset side, but the substitution of the Territorials for the Volunteers, justifiable as it was soon to prove, was not a measure calculated to make a wide appeal, and the same observation may be applied to the measure, already mentioned, which permitted marriage with a deceased wife's sister. In the matter of Ireland, of Education, and of Licensing the Government had definitely failed, owing either to the lack of support for its own Bills or to rejection by the House of Lords. On the other hand, the Trade Disputes Act was decidedly alarming to public opinion. Abroad, too, the situation was not such as to assist Ministers, for the rapid growth of the German Navy placed them on the horns of a dilemma: if they did nothing to reply to this menace they provided their opponents with a very powerful argument, while if they accepted the challenge they would alienate their own Left Wing. As if this were not enough, the agitation for the enfranchisement of women was beginning to assume a violent form, and although this campaign cut across the ordinary party lines it was sufficiently embarrassing to those who were responsible for the government of the country. In short, the administration appeared to be floundering in a sea of difficulties with which it was unable or unwilling to deal, and the electorate, as usual in such circumstances, was turning to the Opposition, divided though this was on more than one important question.

The effect of this was to drive the Government to the Left, and that for more than one reason. In 1908, as we have seen, Mr. Asquith had succeeded Sir Henry Campbell-Bannerman as Prime Minister, and although his views were no more advanced than those of his predecessor his position was not so secure: consequently he had to be more careful not to offend Mr. Lloyd George and the Radical section of his supporters. Furthermore, the momentum which had carried Liberalism to victory in 1906 was clearly dying down, and it could only be revived by some popular appeal. In short, a move had to be made, and with the Whigs gone a move to the Right was out of the question, so a move to the Left it had to be. Such being the case the obvious course to pursue was to direct the party's activities against the House of Lords, as this would unite the various elements that made up the Government's majority. The Liberals had no use for an Upper House which presumed to reject or amend their favourite measures; the Socialists of those days objected to it on principle; and the Irish Nationalists knew that they would never obtain Home Rule while the Lords' veto remained unimpaired.

The situation as it appeared to the Prime Minister and his colleagues in the first weeks of 1909 has been admirably summed up by R. H. Gretton in his *A Modern History of the English People*: "The fight with the House of Lords must be pegged to a single issue, of strong appeal to Labour, and startling. If that House could be lured, by rejecting a Budget, into an assertion of their ultimate power, not merely in ordinary matters of legislation, but in a sphere in which for two hundred years they had admitted a tradition of non-interference, the flagrantly obstinate nature of their party spirit would be displayed. If the Budget could be given a markedly social colour, that obstinacy could be made to appear an entrenched class obstinacy of a kind to rouse even the least politically minded voter to some feeling on a constitutional matter. The taxation of what seemed a peculiarly idle form of capitalistic profit-taking—the increment on land values—for the purpose of establishing new social services, without draining the means for national defence, was a perfect electoral formula".

The so-called "People's Budget", which Mr. Lloyd George introduced in 1909, served this purpose admirably. It was the first Finance Bill deliberately calculated not so much to raise revenue as to produce, in due course, a social revolution, and it made a special appeal to the heterogeneous elements that supported the Government. There was to be a super-tax on incomes over £5,000; death, legacy, and succession duties were to be raised; a levy on unearned increment was proposed; and the Liquor Trade was to be penalized. In defending his proposals the Chancellor of the Exchequer set the tone for the election campaign when he said that it was a war Budget for waging implacable warfare against poverty.

The Budget was fiercely attacked in many quarters, and as the year neared its close the pace of events became accelerated. On November 30th the House of Lords refused to pass the Finance Bill until the electorate had expressed its approval, and three days later Parliament was prorogued. In the interval, however, the Government carried in the Commons, by 349 votes to 134, a motion "That the action of the House of Lords in refusing to pass into law the financial provision made by the House for the service of the year is a breach of the Constitution and a usurpation of the rights of the Commons". This was a skilful move in view of the coming election, for it enlarged the issue from the merits of the Budget to the demerits of the Lords. As the Irish were by no means in agreement with the Liberals and Socialists on the first point, but had no doubts whatever about the second, and as their votes were very necessary to the Government candidates in many constituencies, the resolution was exceedingly well-timed. On December 15th King Edward, acting on the advice of the Prime Minister, dissolved Parliament.

He had, though of course in private, been critical of the Budget proposals from the moment of their conception, and at that time he wrote to Mr. Asquith to enquire whether "in framing the Budget the Cabinet took into consideration the possible (but the King hopes improbably) event of a European War". He then continued, "The Income Tax, which always has been regarded as a war tax, now stands so high for unearned incomes over a certain amount that any great increase would have a most disastrous effect on land generally, more especially if the war lasted for a considerable time". If the King was distrustful of the merits of the Budget, he cordially disliked the terms in which it was recommended to the electorate by some members of the Government, and Mr. L. Harcourt in particular was admonished for referring to the Peers as "assassins".

The King was under no illusions concerning the seriousness of the constitutional crisis which loomed ahead, and his pre-occupation was to ensure a peaceful settlement. First of all, he ascertained the views of the two parties while the Budget was yet under consideration by the Upper House.

At the end of September the First Lord of the Admiralty, Mr. Reginald McKenna, pointed out to King Edward that the rejection of the measure by the Lords would be a violent breach of the established constitutional practice, and would call for an immediate definition and limitation of their powers by statute. No two principles, he urged, were more firmly settled in the Constitution than that the House of Commons is alone responsible for taxation, and that it is only by a vote of the Lower House that the life of the government of the day can be terminated. Yet the action of the Lords in rejecting a Finance Bill would amount to a denial of both these principles, and no government could remain in office unless it were guaranteed against similar action by the Lords in future. He pointed out that the rejection of a Finance Bill differed greatly from the rejection of any other Bill, in that unless such a measure was passed every year the administration of the national services could not proceed, and as a Finance Bill must be passed annually, the Lords could force an election in any year they pleased. He pointed out that a Finance Bill had never yet been thrown out by the Lords, and that the rejection of the present one would be "the first step in a revolution".

The Conservative leaders were equally uncompromising. Lord Cawdor, for example, wrote to the

King that "the object of the second Chamber is that it should secure to the electors of the country the opportunity of exercising their wishes as to important legislative proposals before they become law", and he expressed the opinion that proposals in the Finance Bill made it difficult to justify the passing of such proposals into law without giving the people an opportunity of exercising their views upon them. "For this purpose the House of Lords need not express any view, favourable or unfavourable, to the Budget proposals". The reference of such an important Bill to the electorate seemed to Lord Cawdor to be one of the primary duties of the House of Lords. As these views were shared by Lord Lansdowne and Mr. Balfour there was clearly nothing for the King to do but to see if the result of the General Election would do anything to clear the air.

This was exactly what did not happen. When the final results were announced it was found that the Liberal majority of 1906 had disappeared, and in the new House of Commons the strength of the parties was: Conservatives 242, Liberal-Unionists 31, Liberals 275, Socialists 40, Irish Nationalists 81. The Government losses were almost entirely confined to England, where the Conservatives and Liberal-Unionists even had a slight majority over all their opponents.

This result raised problems of the first magnitude. Had the Government received a mandate from the electors to force the Budget through the House of Lords? The Liberals maintained that such was clearly the case since the Conservatives were in a minority in the new House, but to this it was objected that the Irish were opposed to the Budget, and that if they voted according to their convictions the administration would be in a minority. The difficulty of their position was realized by some members of the Government, and the Prime Minister informed the King that a section of the Cabinet was of the opinion that "in view of the exorbitant demands of Mr. Redmond and his followers, and the impossibility under existing Parliamentary conditions of counting upon a stable Government majority, the wisest and most dignified course for Ministers was at once to tender their resignation to Your Majesty". The Irish, in effect, were prepared to vote for the Budget, but they demanded a preliminary assurance that once it was passed legislation would immediately be introduced to remove the veto of the House of Lords so that a measure of Home Rule could be carried, if necessary, over the head of that body. For a moment the Cabinet hesitated, and then it decided to remain in office. Mr. Redmond was told he could turn it out if he dared, which he could not afford to do, as the Prime Minister knew very well, and with the opening of Parliament in February, 1910, the conflict entered upon a new phase.

Once Mr. Asquith had made up his mind not to resign he lost no time in rallying a majority. On March 21st he tabled three resolutions: the first declared it expedient that the House of Lords should be prevented from rejecting or amending money Bills; the second stipulated that if a Bill passed the Commons in three successive Sessions, and was thrice rejected by the Lords it should "become law without the consent of the House of Lords on the Royal assent being declared"; and the third limited the duration of any one Parliament to five years, thus modifying the Septennial Act of 1716. These resolutions were carried by April 14th, and the Prime Minister then introduced a Bill founded on them. Meanwhile, negotiations had been taking place with Mr. Redmond: a few changes were made in the Finance Bill to render it more palatable to Ireland, and, as the House of Lords made no further resistance, it became law at the end of April.

In the meantime King Edward had propounded some views of his own with regard to the House of Lords, and coming from one of such wide political experience they possess more than a merely ephemeral interest. In conversation with Lord Crewe, then Colonial Secretary, at Windsor he said that he was quite convinced that it was wiser to take the House of Lords as it was, and to make use of the large amount of good material there, rather than to attempt to create a new chamber. He suggested, therefore, that the House should remain exactly as it was for every purpose except that of voting. Every peer would have his seat in the House, and be entitled to speak if he desired, but only one hundred would be able to vote: these hundred would be nominated by the leaders of the Conservative and Liberal parties respectively for the term of a Parliament. After some further conversation the King asked Lord Crewe to think the proposal over carefully, and he promised to discuss it with him again later in the year. Lord Crewe left it on record that "during the conversation I had with His Majesty I was impressed by his shrewd appreciation of the difficulties surrounding the creation of a new Second Chamber, difficulties which were thoroughly realised when, several years later, the whole subject was for the first time closely examined by the joint Conference of both Houses, presided over by Lord Bryce".

Nothing came of this conversation, and an immediate constitutional crisis on a scale which had been unparalleled since the days of the Reform Bill in 1832 seemed inevitable, when, on May 6th, 1910, King Edward VII died.

His successor, King George V, was not very widely known, though he had not been kept in the back-ground, nor had he had the disagreements with his father which had become almost a tradition in the Royal Family for the past two hundred years. As a younger son he had been brought up as a naval officer, and he was already in the late twenties when the death of the Duke of Clarence made him heir to the throne. In that capacity he had done his duty conscientiously, and of his devotion to his father there was never any question. At the same time it would be idle to pretend that on his accession he was popular, and there were ugly rumours, to which in his later years he would jokingly refer, that he was unduly addicted to the bottle. Furthermore, there were many who shook their heads over the prospect of a naval officer on the throne, and who cited the precedents of James II and William IV in support of their apprehensions.

As time was to show, King George V was one of that numerous class of men who mature late. In this, as in much else, he inherited the Coburg characteristics of his paternal grandfather. There are two strains in the British Royal Family, Hanover and Coburg, and in most of its members one or the other of these strains is dominant. Perhaps, indeed, the Hanoverian characteristics can themselves be subdivided. First of all there is the dull, sadistic type, insensible to the finer things of life, personified in the first two Georges, the Butcher Duke of Cumberland, and Queen Victoria's "wicked uncle Ernest", subsequently King of Hanover. Then there is the more mercurial, and slightly more attractive, if wholly irresponsible, type exemplified by Frederick, Prince of Wales, George IV, and, among the females, his daughter, Charlotte. Coburg was quite different, being wholly unimaginative, but extremely conscientious, and in no way given to the eccentricities that marked so many members of the House of Hanover. Of the views of King George V on the subject of the influence of

heredity there is probably no record, but if he had
time during those busy May days in 1910 to reflect
upon his immediate predecessors on the throne he must
have done so with very mixed feelings.

The founder of the dynasty, George I, was probably
the least attractive. Lady Mary Wortley Montagu
wrote of him, "He could speak no English, and was
past the age of learning. Our customs and laws were
all mysteries to him, which he neither tried to understand, nor was capable of understanding if he
endeavoured it". Lord Chesterfield was even more
outspoken: "The King loved pleasure, and was not
delicate in his choice of it. No woman came amiss to
him, if they were very willing and very fat . . . the
standard of His Majesty's taste made all those ladies
who aspired to his favour, and who were near the
statutable size, strain and swell themselves like the
frogs in the fable to rival the bulk and dignity of the
ox. Some succeeded, and others burst". Perhaps,
however, the French ambassador provided the real
clue when he wrote of George I, "He rather considers
England as a temporary possession to be made the
most of while it lasts, than as a perpetual inheritance
for himself and his family".

The woman who should have been the first
Hanoverian Queen of England, Sophia Dorothea of
Celle, had been divorced by her husband in 1694 on a
charge of adultery with Konigsmarck, whom the
Jacobites alleged to be the father of George II. Her
fate, which recalls that of her great-granddaughter,
the unhappy wife of Christian VII of Denmark, was one
of the most cruel in modern history. She was little more
than a girl when the tribunal that pronounced
sentence of divorce debarred her from ever marrying
again, though leaving George at liberty to do so. For
the remaining thirty-two years of her life she was

confined to the castle of Ahlden, which is situated in the dreary plains of North Germany, where she was cut off from all society of her own age and rank; she was not allowed to see her children, and when her son, later George II, attempted to gain access to his mother, he was forcibly prevented. The wretched woman died in 1726, and the severity of her husband pursued her even after death. He ordered that she should be buried in the garden of Ahlden, but the place was little better than a swamp, and when three attempts had been made to dig a grave which would not instantly fill with water, she was perforce buried in consecrated ground.

Nemesis, however, was not slow to overtake George I. On the 17th of June in the following year he landed in Holland on his way to Hanover for the first time since his wife's death. Her one faithful servant met him on the German frontier, and gave him a message traced by her dying hand summoning him to meet her before the Judgment Seat of God. Then, as if pursued by the Furies, came the headlong journey of the stricken man—"to Osnabruck, to Osnabruck!"— and there he died before midnight, as if impelled to hasten without delay to keep that awful tryst.

George II had been to some extent an improvement on his father, with whom he was, of course, always on the worst of terms, but his first appearance as King was not impressive. On June 24th (Old Style) 1727 he was alseep after dinner at Richmond Lodge, when a man entered his room, and knelt before him in his jackboots. George asked him with the strongest of German accents who had dared to disturb his repose. "I am Sir Robert Walpole", was the reply, "I have the honour to announce to Your Majesty that Your Royal father, King George I, died at Osnabruck on Saturday last, the 10th instant". To which the new monarch answered, "Dat is one big lie". Certainly humour was not one of the more prominent characteristics of George II. He was at the play on one occasion in his later years, and during the course of it one of the characters, an intriguing chambermaid, said to an old gentleman, "You are villainously old; you are sixty-six; you can't have the impudence to think of living above two years". At this the King was heard to exclaim in a passion, "This is damned stuff".

It would, however, be a mistake to dismiss George II merely as an active, if fussy, little man, of no inconsiderable personal courage. There was a darker side to his character, and he was the true father of the Butcher Duke of Cumberland; the Forty-Five showed him in his true colours as one to whom the word mercy had no meaning. The Queen, Caroline of Anspach, was a very capable woman, but she died in 1737, that is to say twenty-three years before her husband.

Their eldest son Frederick, Prince of Wales, was loathed by his parents with a hatred which is quite inexplicable by any fact of which we are in possession. He was certainly weak and foolish, and he was capable on occasions of that outrageous behaviour character-istic of the whole Hanoverian dynasty. When his wife was seized with the first pangs of childbirth at Hampton Court he insisted on removing her to St. James's for her confinement in spite both of her entreaties and of the danger involved. During the last fourteen years of his life the Prince was in open conflict with his father. The King banished him from Court, and refused to receive anybody who visited his son. According to Lord Harvey the Queen said of Frederick, "My dear firstborn is the greatest ass, and the greatest liar, and the greatest canaille and the greatest beast in the whole world, and I most heartily wish he was out of it". Not to be outdone, the Prince, when he received the bulletins announcing his mother's impending

75

death, observed, "Well, now we shall have some good news; she cannot hold out much longer".

The only light that is thrown upon the real cause of this unedifying quarrel is provided by a memorandum of Lord Hardwicke, the Lord Chancellor: "Sir Robert Walpole informed me of certain passages between the King and himself, and between the King and the Prince, of too high and secret a nature even to be trusted to this narrative; but from thence I found great reason to think that this unhappy difference between the King and Queen and His Royal Highness turned upon some points of a more interesting and important nature than have hitherto appeared".

With the accession of George III the monarchy became more dignified, and that monarch's efforts to maintain the power of the Crown have been discussed on an earlier page. On the other hand George III introduced insanity into the Royal Family. There had clearly been a streak of abnormality in the Guelphs from the beginning. No normal man could have behaved as George I did to his wife, or George II to his son; sadism was the most prominent characteristic of the Butcher Duke of Cumberland; while the behaviour of the Queen of Denmark, the sister of George III, argues some degree of nymphomania. In the next generation few would describe George IV as completely balanced. It is to be noted that George III displayed symptoms of his malady more than once before he finally became hopelessly insane. He had shown signs of madness for a few weeks in 1765, but in the autumn of 1788 he went definitely out of his mind. He had been in failing health throughout the previous summer, and is said, while driving in Windsor Park, to have alighted and shaken hands with the branch of an oak tree under the impression that it was the King of Prussia. In a few weeks, however, he was completely restored to health.

The final relapse in 1811 was probably due to a variety of causes. One was the death of his favourite daughter, the Princess Amelia, and the other was the disgrace of one of his sons, the Duke of York. A further factor was almost certainly the failure of the expedition to Walcheren. So George III passed out of history, and spent the remaining nine years of his life at Windsor. He was still able to find some solace in music, especially in Handel, and he chose for the anthems in his chapel all the passages from that composer connected with blindness and madness.

Of his successor as a monarch something has been said in an earlier chapter; of George IV as a man the opinion of his contemporaries was overwhelmingly unfavourable. The Duke of Wellington, whose loyalty to the throne was above suspicion, said, "He speaks so like old Falstaff, that, damn me, if I was not afraid to walk into a room with him"; and in the year of his accession, 1820, the Duke declared him "degraded as low as he could be already". George also, especially in his later years, suffered from delusions, which at times were a source of considerable annoyance to those with whom he was brought into contact. He fancied that he had led the Heavy Dragoons at Salamanca, and that he had ridden Fleur-de-Lys at Goodwood. Nor were his habits any more attractive than his character. He was want to give way on occasion to outbreaks of maudlin sentimentality, when he would weep on his ministers' shoulders, and even kiss the Duke of Wellington on the cheek. Canning, too, whom George never appreciated, was compelled to submit to these familiarities, and on at least one occasion he had to walk along the front at Brighton with the King's arm round his neck.

In the later years of his reign George IV withdrew from the public gaze, and became more indolent than ever, rarely rising before six o'clock in the evening, and receiving his ministers in night-attire. When Goderich resigned and Wellington was summoned to form a ministry, the new Premier found the King in bed "dressed in a dirty silk jacket and a turban nightcap, one as greasy as the other; for, notwithstanding his coquetry about dress in public, he was extremely dirty and slovenly in private". Such was the so-called First Gentleman of Europe, a term that might have been applied with considerably more reason to either of the French monarchs who were his contemporaries.

It is little wonder that Walter Savage Landor should have written:

I sing the Georges four,
For Providence could stand no more.
Some say that far the worst
Of all the four was George the First.
But yet by some 'tis reckoned,
That worse still was George the Second.
And what mortal ever heard,
Any good of George the Third?
When George the Fourth from earth descended,
Thank God the line of Georges ended.

The careers of these, his ancestors, can hardly fail to have been present to the mind of their successor, King George V, when his turn came to follow them on the throne. As he looked at the living members of the Royal Family he must at times have wondered to what extent they were likely to be subject, for better or for worse, to the operation of the laws of heredity. Above all there were the disturbing precedents of the relations of the reigning monarch with the heir apparent which dated from the arrival of the dynasty from Hanover nearly two hundred years before. He himself, in his devotion to his father, had proved the solitary exception, but was the old dismal story of dissension between the King of England and the Prince of Wales to be repeated once more? Time alone could show.

One personal unpleasantness the new King very soon had to suffer. A certain Edward Mylius, in a paper called the *Liberator*, published an article giving fresh currency to an old rumour that King George V, before marrying Queen Mary, had as a naval officer contracted a marriage at Malta with an admiral's daughter. Mylius was duly put on trial, but, confronted in the conduct of his defence with the constitutional impossibility of calling the King in evidence, he gave up his case and was sentenced to twelve months' imprisonment. After the sentence, when no constitutional point could be involved, the Attorney-General read in court, by the King's direction, an explicit denial of the rumours, thereby displaying not only a realization of the prevalence of the story, but also a determination that no one in future should be able to say that, though the offence of publication had been dealt with, the point of fact remained obscure behind a constitutional formality.

Meanwhile, the accession of King George V had diverted public attention from political controversy, and when the ceremonies connected with it and with the funeral of his predecessor were over there was a general feeling that it would be most unfair to confront the new monarch with a constitutional crisis. If the politicians could arrive at a compromise between themselves, the ordinary citizen argued, it would be better for everybody. Accordingly the Prime Minister proposed to Mr. Balfour that four of the leading men on either side should meet in conference with a view to finding a solution acceptable to both parties. The Opposition leader agreed to the proposal, and Mr. Asquith nominated to represent the Government, in addition to himself, the Marquess of Crewe, Mr. Lloyd George, and Mr. Birrell, while Mr. Balfour chose the Marquess of Lansdowne, Earl Cawdor, and Mr. Austen Chamberlain. To this day it is not easy to decide whether the Prime Minister really wanted a compromise or was merely playing for time, though there would appear to be little doubt that Mr. Lloyd George was sincerely desirous of an agreement.

The conference met for the first time on June 17th, 1910, and it continued to sit, with several interruptions, until November 10th, holding twenty-two meetings in all. To quote Austen Chamberlain: "There were times when we seemed very near agreement on some aspects of the problem, such, for instance, as the treatment of financial measures and general legislation, but the shadow of the Home Rule controversy hung over us all. The Unionists contended that organic measures, that is measures affecting the Crown and the Constitution, must be subject to special safeguards, ensuring that, if the two Houses disagreed, the nation should be consulted before they became irrevocable. As to the Crown and the Constitutional Act which would result from any agreement we might reach, there was, I believe, no insuperable difference, but Home Rule barred the way. On this point we could obtain no satisfaction. . . ." One particularly interesting feature of the conference was that evidence was taken as to constitutional practice in the United States and Canada, and Dr. Murray Butler, President of Columbia University, and Mr. Fielding, of Canada, appeared to explain the position in their respective countries.

On November 10th the last meeting of the conference was held, and its definite failure was admitted. Actually it had to all intents and purposes broken down nearly a month before over the treatment of Home Rule Bills. Mr. Balfour had proposed that if such measures were twice rejected they should become the subject of a plebiscite, but although Mr. Lloyd George admitted this was reasonable he said it was impossible for the Government to agree to it. On November 10th, however, the Prime Minister put forward the proposal that a General Election should intervene on the next occasion on which a Home Rule Bill passed the House of Commons, was rejected by the Lords, but in this one case only, and that in future Home Rule Bills were to be treated in the ordinary way like any other measure. For the rest, the Government proposed that if a difference arose between Lords and Commons on two occasions in two sessions in two years it was to be settled by a joint sitting of the two Houses; this was to consist of the whole of the House of Commons and one hundred peers, twenty of whom were to be Government supporters and eighty were to be selected on a system of proportional representation.

As to financial legislation, the Budget was not to be rejected by the Lords except in case of tacking, which was to be defined as follows: "Finance is the sole business of the House of Commons, provided that it appears that any provisions of a Bill, though dealing with taxation, would effect important social or political changes through expropriation or different-iation against any class or owners of property these provisions shall not be treated for the purposes of this Act as provisions dealing with taxation". In that event the Government would have to embody such proposals in an ordinary Bill, to which the normal procedure would apply. The decision as to what was, and what was not, a geniune money Bill was to rest with a joint committee of the two Houses, composed of seven from each elected at the beginning of every Parliament, presided over by the Speaker with a casting vote only. In the matter of constitutional legislation Mr. Asquith said that no discrimination could be considered, but his Government was willing to agree that Bills affecting the Crown or the Protestant Succession should be subject to special safeguards, that is to say, if the two Houses differed they should be dropped, but otherwise they should go to a plebiscite. After the last session of the conference there was a meeting of the Opposition leaders at Lansdowne House, when it was decided that these suggestions did not provide a satisfactory basis for a compromise.

This conference, like so many similar gatherings, was less remarkable for what took place at its formal sessions than for what went on behind the scenes. In this instance it was no less than a proposal by Mr. Lloyd George for the formation of a Coalition administration. The suggestion was never discussed in the conference itself, and it was first made by the Chancellor of the Exchequer to Mr. Balfour in terms of such secrecy that the Conservative leader did not at first mention it to his colleagues, though it was subsequently ascertained that the Prime Minister knew all about the proposals from the beginning. Before the negotiations finally broke down the matter had been disclosed to the other five members of the conference as well as to Mr. Winston Churchill, Mr. Bonar Law, Mr. F. E. Smith, Mr. Akers-Douglas, and Mr. Gerald Balfour. The rank and file of the two parties concerned had, of course, no idea of what was afoot, and Mr. Austen Chamberlain was fully justified in his comment, "What a world we live in, and how the public would stare if they could look into our minds, and our letter-bags".

In brief, the Chancellor of the Exchequer argued that, while parties would always disagree on certain vital issues, at that moment the most important questions were capable of being settled by the action of the two great parties without any sacrifice of principle on the part of either. The progress of events abroad had rendered the matter urgent, and the problems which this new situation raised could not be dealt with by a single party without its incurring a load of temporary unpopularity within its own ranks which neither side could afford to face if it stood alone, confronted by an Opposition ready to take every advantage of tripping it up. The examples given were: housing, the sale of drink, insurance, unemployment, the Poor Law, and national reorganization, including under this head national defence (for which the Swiss militia system was suggested as a model), trade and tariffs, and schemes for uniting the Empire and utilizing its resources for defence as well as for commerce and foreign policy.

So far did these negotiations go at one moment that the actual distirbution of offices in the Coalition Government was considered. Mr. Lloyd George suggested that Mr. Asquith should become First Lord of the Treasury with a peerage, Mr. Balfour President of the Committee of Defence with the leadership of the Commons, Lord Lansdowne Foreign Secretary, and Mr. Austen Chamberlain First Lord of the Admiralty; Mr. Lloyd George was to remain Chancellor of the Exchequer, but he expressed his willingness to vacate that office in favour of Mr. Chamberlain. This grandiose scheme, however, came to nothing. It would have necessitated each side doing what it most disliked to please the other, and there was no compelling motive to bring the parties together as was to be the case five years later. In particular, the concessions required from the Opposition in the matter of Home Rule, Welsh Disestablishment, and Education were greater than the rank and file throughout the country would have been prepared to accept.

It has been necessary to discuss these events in some detail, partly because the meeting of the conference was in itself caused by the change of monarch, and partly because its failure was to be attended by circumstances which led to serious criticism of the conduct of King George V by one section of his subjects.

The political truce came to an end at the beginning of November, 1910, and on the 11th of that month it was announced that the conference had broken up without reaching any agreement, though nothing was said as to the causes of its failure. Four days later Parliament met, and the Veto Bill was introduced in the House of Lords. Its terms were that, pending a reform of the composition of the Upper Chamber, any measure which passed the Commons in three successive sessions unchanged might be presented for the Royal Assent without the consent of the Lords; and that any financial measure might be put before the King in the same way if, at the end of a month, the Lords' consent was withheld. The Government did not wait for the Bill to be defeated, for a week after the failure of the conference the announcement of the coming dissolution of Parliament was made. In making it the Prime Minister repeated a statement which he had made just before the death of King Edward to the effect that, in the event of the issue being further forced, he would not advise a dissolution except on such conditions as would enable him, if successful at the polls, to place the Veto Bill (as the Parliament Bill was generally called) upon the statute-book despite the resistance of the House of Lords. This could only mean that if the Government won the election, and the Lords still refused to give way, Mr. Asquith had received from the new King the assurance that sufficient peers would be created to ensure the passage of the Bill.

This announcement gave rise to a storm of adverse criticism of the King in Conservative circles, where he was accused of having allowed the Crown to become an instrument of Liberal policy. Nor was this charge wholly unfounded, for there was another course which he might, with perfect constitutional propriety, have taken, and that was to have entrusted Mr. Balfour with the formation of an administration. The reason this was not done was because the King was given to understand that the Conservative Leader would not take office, though he does not seem to have made any very determined effort to find out for himself, and he would appear to have relied upon information which was far from disinterested. It is true that the Opposition had no desire to take office, but it would certainly have done so in such circumstances. A General Election would, of course, have been necessary, but the result might have been very different from what it subsequently proved to be had the issue been the propriety of creating peers to enable Home Rule to be carried without the definite approval of the electorate. Had Mr. Balfour been beaten at the polls the House of Lords must have accepted the verdict, and the threat to swamp that body by the creation of new peers would not have been necessary. In effect, whichever way the nation voted, the crisis of the following year would have been avoided; that it took place was thus to no inconsiderable extent due to this misinterpretation of the situation on the part of the King.

The General Election of December, 1910, decided nothing. No less than 87 per cent of those who were in a position to vote did so, as compared with 92 per cent in the previous January, and there were returned 240 Conservatives, 34 Liberal-Unionists, 270 Liberals, 42 Socialists, and 84 Irish Nationalists. This verdict was extremely unsatisfactory, for the fact that the Conservatives and Unionists were slightly superior in numbers to the Liberals encouraged their Right Wing to oppose the Veto Bill to the uttermost, and for several months it looked as if the King might be called upon to fulfil his promise to create enough peers to ensure the passage of the measure through the Upper House.

The new Parliament met on February 6th, 1911, and on the 21st the Prime Minister introduced the Veto Bill. For the next six months tempers at Westminster became steadily more inflamed, but the constitutional crisis of 1911 was, it may be observed, in no sense a national crisis, for the nation as a whole took little interest in it. There were several reasons for this. It was the year of the Coronation, and the pageantry which attended that event naturally made a greater appeal to the man in the street than an arid controversy regarding the powers of the House of Lords. Then, again, the months when the political struggle was being waged most strenuously witnessed a number of events calculated to arrest public attention. Such were the "battle of Sidney Street", the Clapham Common Murder, the formal inauguration of the Queen Victoria Memorial with the new Mall and the Admiralty Arch, and the production of "Kismet". Save at rare intervals, these, and the heat which made the summer of 1911 the hottest of the century, distracted the popular notice from politics, and, as was certainly not the case in 1832, it was against a background of general indifference that the battle over the latest change in the Constitution was fought.

The Veto Bill, having been forced through the Commons, reached the Upper House in May. Earlier in the month the Marquess of Lansdowne, on behalf of the Opposition had produced a scheme for the reform of the House of Lords, and for this prospectively reformed Chamber he now attempted to retain power by amendments to the Veto Bill: these provided for a Joint Committee of both Houses in matters of disagreement, and reserved for a Referendum such Bills as those "establishing national Parliaments" or "raising issues of great gravity". It was clear that the Government would not accept these amendments, and the question at once arose whether the Opposition majority in the House of Lords would insist on them, and thus force the creation of peers. The issue was not at once joined, for the Coronation took place on June 22nd, but on July 21st a letter from the Prime Minister to Mr. Balfour was published stating that the Commons would be asked to disagree with the Lords' amendments, and proceeding, "In the circumstances, should the necessity arise, the Government will advise the King to exercise his Prerogative to secure the passing into law of the Bill in substantially the same form in which it left the House of Commons, and His Majesty has been pleased to signify that he will consider it his duty to accept the act on that advice".

This letter was the occasion of one of the stormiest scenes in British Parliamentary History. When, on the 24th, Mr. Asquith rose to move the rejection of the Lords amendments, and to make his statement, the Opposition refused him a hearing. He was howled down, and the Speaker adjourned the House without question put. All the same a solution was very near. On the following day another letter was published, this time from Mr. Balfour to Lord Newton, and in it the Conservative leader advised the House of Lords to accept the original Bill, and to abandon their amendments. His advice was taken and the end came on August 11th, when the Bill passed the Lords by 131 votes to 114.

The first great crisis of the reign was over.

IV

KING GEORGE V (continued)

Disturbed Condition of the Country—Foreign Complications—The King and the Continent—The Home Rule Controversy—Intervention of King George—The Buckingham Palace Conference—The First World War and the Monarchy—Attitude of the King— His Views—Post-war Complications—Mr. Asquith's Miscalculation—The King's Illness—Its Effect on His Popularity—The Crisis of 1931—King George's Part— Formation of the National Government—Misdirected Criticism—The Silver Jubilee— Death of King George V—His Place in History

IT MIGHT have been supposed that the passage into law of the Veto Bill would have been followed by a period of calm in which the rival parties would have licked their wounds while reflecting upon the danger of pushing their theories to extremes, but King George V was not destined to have any such respite. The three years which elapsed before the outbreak of the First World War were marked by a violence in the political and social life of the country for which it is necessary to go back exactly two centuries to find a parallel. On all sides there was a lack of restraint in language and conduct, and a tendency to resort to force as the one unanswerable argument. While the constitutional struggle was still in progress, and the pageantry of the Coronation was yet fresh in the public memory, the troubles had already begun. At various ports the seamen came out on strike in June; carters and vanmen struck in July; and in August there was a strike of the London dockers. Everywhere these disputes were accompanied by violence. At Hull and

Cardiff there was fighting in the streets; also at Manchester, where the authorities had been compelled to send for a strong force of London police and for the Scots Greys from the garrison at York. There were the most violent scenes in Liverpool, where the troops were compelled to open fire with the result that two men were shot dead, and two hundred people were injured. Meanwhile, there had been a railway strike, which failed chiefly because motor transport, although still in its infancy, was already providing an alternative mode of transport to the railways. It is true that the summer had been exceptionally hot, but that was not the only reason for frayed tempers, as coming events were to prove.

The bitterness with which every industrial dispute was contested at this period is well illustrated by an event in the following year when Ben Tillett got a big meeting of strikers on Tower Hill to repeat after him, "Oh, God, strike Lord Devonport dead". Nor were political agitators behind their industrial fellows in the adoption of methods which horrified those who had passed the greater part of their lives in the calm of the later nineteenth century. The suffragettes, in particular, stopped at nothing, and the more repressive the Government's measures the more active they became. A bomb in St. John's Church, Westminster, blew out a stained-glass window just after evening service one Sunday; another was found under the Coronation Chair in Westminster Abbey; and a third in St. George's, Hanover Square. Wargrave Church was burned to the ground. The King was assailed with shouted appeals at the charity *matinée*, and at one of the Courts a lady in the act of curtseying shouted, "Your Majesty, won't you stop torturing women?" At the Derby in 1913 a militant who had been more than once in prison dashed out on the course in front of the horses as they came round Tattenham Corner, and was so crushed that she died within a few hours. Between 1911 and 1914 there was little of that restraint which is commonly associated with English public life.

Abroad the situation was no different, and Europe was already on the slippery slope. In September, 1911, Italy seized the Ottoman Vilayet of Tripoli for no obvious reason, but in reality to forestall similar action on the part of any other Power. The following year saw the collapse of the Turks before the armies of the Balkan States, and its successor witnessed the victors fighting one another for the spoils. Above all, there was the growing menace of Germany, and her evident intention to strike for the hegemony of the Continent. The Government, not without pressure from the Opposition, was substantially increasing the Navy, but to many that was not enough, and Lord Roberts began to conduct an energetic campaign in favour of National Service. Yet the country as a whole was not aware of any impending danger. Nearly a hundred years had elapsed since England had fought in Western Europe; only a few old men remembered the Crimea; and recent wars, not excluding the struggle in South Africa, had hardly affected the national life. For a moment, in the summer of 1911, when Germany sent a warship to Morocco, which was practically a French possession, there was widespread alarm, but nothing happened, and the excitement speedily died down.

The general unrest, both at home and abroad, explains much of the political situation that would otherwise be inexplicable. The Opposition considered that the methods employed to put the Veto Bill upon the Statute Book, as well as that Bill itself, had strained the Constitution almost to breaking-point, and that they were accordingly justified in adopting tactics which might otherwise not have been admissible. Smarting under the loss of three successive General Elections, they felt that Tierney's famous definition of the duty of an Opposition admirably fitted their own case, namely to propose nothing, to oppose everything, and to turn out the Government. No handle against the administration was to be neglected, and this explains why such measures as the Insurance Bill, which in retrospect appears almost noncontentious, were so fiercely attacked. How seriously the man-in-the-street took all this it is difficult to say. He was certainly more interested in politics than he was later to become, and it must be confessed that from a spectacular point of view politics were decidedly attractive. On the Government side, a speech by Mr. Lloyd George or Mr. Winston Churchill was always good value in vituperation and personalities, while it was sure within a few days to produce, on the part of the Opposition, a retort by Sir Edward Carson or Mr. F. E. Smith couched in similar language. On the other hand, those who preferred to see the controversy carried on at a higher level had their choice of Mr. Asquith or Mr. Balfour. Political warfare was almost gladiatorial, and one is sometimes tempted to the conclusion that contemporaries regarded it as such rather than the serious affair it had been in the days of their fathers.

As has already been suggested, King George V, like his predecessor, was inclined to regard a great many of the questions about which the politicians got excited as being of a parish-pump character, though the growing violence in word and deed occasioned him considerable concern. He had, it is true, a short respite from constitutional worries once the Parliament Act was an accomplished fact, and he utilized this not only to get to know something at first hand of conditions in Great

Britain, but also to visit Ireland and India. There can be no doubt that during these three years of peace both the King and the Queen did much to live down the unpopularity which attached to them in some quarters when they came to the throne, and they laid the foundations of that affection and respect which were to be of inestimable value to the monarchy in the difficult times that lay ahead.

In one respect there was a marked departure from the practice of the previous reign, and it was in the new King's lack of interest in foreign affairs. He made no attempt to play any part in Continental politics, and the interchange of visits with contemporary rulers was limited to the minimum that convention demanded. The reasons for this probably are that King George shared to the full his subjects' prejudice against all foreigners, and also that he doubted his ability to hold his own in their company in the way that his father had done. He read far more widely than King Edward, but conscientious and honourable as he was by nature, there was nothing of the diplomat about him; as he was to show in the case of his sons, he had little idea of the way to handle men. Nor is there any reason to suppose that King George's knowledge of the intricacies of the international situation was particularly profound, and his recorded comments on the murder of the Archduke Franz Ferdinand give no indication that he realized this event might have important repercussions. He would not appear to have grasped what was really at stake. All this meant a further limitation of the power of the Crown, in fact if not in theory, and it is the more to be regretted because there is always the chance that if the King of England at that time had carried more weight in the counsels of Europe the tragic events of 1914 might have taken a different course.

However this may be, the King was thoroughly alive to the growing danger of civil war at home as the Home Rule controversy aroused a bitterness in political circles in England for which it would have been difficult to find a parallel in recent history. Writing in his *Life of John Redmond* of the position in the spring of 1914 Mr. Denis Gwynn says, "It was well known, and not least to Redmond, that for months the King had been urged on all sides, by many influential advisers, to exercise his latent powers under the Constitution. Various proposals had been vehemently advocated in the newspapers: that the King should either force a dissolution, or insist upon a referendum on the Home Rule Bill, or even exercise the prerogative of dismissing his Ministers, which had not been used since 1834. Some had even suggested that the King should address a letter to his subjects explaining the grounds on which he was to intervene".

No such dramatic intervention by the Crown took place, but the following letter was in due course sent to Mr. Asquith:

Buckingham Palace.
18th July, 1914.

My dear Prime Minister,

The situation has indeed become, as you say in your letter of this morning just received, one of such grave national emergency that I cordially welcome your advice that I should intervene before the crisis becomes more acute. I therefore authorize you to announce that I will invite representatives of parties, British and Irish, to a conference, with a view of determining a settlement of the outstanding issues so clearly explained in your letter.

I appreciate the difficulties that may be felt by some in acceding to my request. But I rejoice to think that I shall secure the attendance of the distinguished representatives of the parties concerned.

It is a pleasure to me that the conference will take place

in my house, where I shall gladly welcome its members on Tuesday, the 21st instant, at an hour convenient to them.

I feel confident by thus meeting my wishes a great advance will be made towards a friendly understanding, which, please God, may result in averting the dangers which threaten the welfare of not only the United Kingdom but of my whole Empire.

Yours etc.

George R.I.

On the morning of the day suggested, namely July 21st, the conference duly met at Buckingham Palace, and it was composed of the Prime Minister and Mr. Lloyd George; Lord Lansdowne and Mr. Bonar Law; Mr. Redmond and Mr. Dillon; Sir Edward Carson and Mr. Craig. They were received by the King, who welcomed each member separately; after this, the members of the conference took their seats round the Council Room table. King George was in the chair, and he opened proceedings with this speech:

Gentlemen,

It is with feelings of satisfaction and hopefulness that I receive you here to-day, and I thank you for the manner in which you have responded to my summons. It is also a matter of congratulation that the Speaker has consented to preside over your meetings.

My intervention at this moment may be regarded as a new departure, but the exceptional circumstances under which you are brought together justify my action.

For months we have watched with deep misgivings the course of events in Ireland. The trend has been surely and steadily towards an appeal to force, and to-day the cry of civil war is on the lips of the most responsible and sober-minded of my people.

We have in the past endeavoured to act as a civilizing example to the world, and to me it is unthinkable, as it must be to you, that we should be brought to the brink of fratricidal strife upon issues apparently so capable of adjustment as those you are now asked to consider, if handled in a spirit of generous compromise.

My apprehension in contemplating such a dire calamity is intensified by my feelings of attachment to Ireland and of sympathy with her people, who have always welcomed me with warm-hearted affection.

Gentlemen, you represent in one form or another the vast majority of my subjects at home. You also have a deep interest in my Dominions over sea, who are scarcely less concerned in a prompt and friendly settlement of this question.

I regard you then in this matter as trustees for the honour and peace of all.

Your responsibilities are indeed great. The time is short. You will, I know, employ it to the fullest advantage, and be patient, earnest and conciliatory, in view of the magnitude of the interests at stake. I pray that God in His infinite wisdom may guide your deliberations so that they may result in the joy of peace and honourale settlement.

The King, it may be added, then left the room, and the Speaker took the chair.

The intervention of the Crown was not destined to be successful. On July 24th the Prime Minister announced in the House of Commons that the conference had been unable to come to any agreement "either in principle or in detail". It seemed impossible to avoid catastrophe, for within a few weeks the Home Rule Bill would become law. Two days after Mr. Asquith had spoken the Nationalists landed a big consignment of arms near Howth, while, on the other side, arrangements were being hurriedly made for opening English country houses to women and children from Ulster as soon as the fighting should begin. Such was the state of British politics when, on July 28th, the Foreign Secretary rose in the Commons to make a statement concerning the Austrian rejection of Serbia's reply to an ultimatum demanding satisfaction for the murder of the Archduke Franz Ferdinand.

It is not easy to decide whether the First World War, which in general dealt a very severe blow at the monarchical principle, strengthened or weakened the British monarchy. On what may perhaps be described as the debit side was the fact that the new military formations were termed Kitchener's Army, while it is difficult to resist the conclusion that the change of the name of the reigning dynasty was an unworthy concession to popular hysteria, and it gave rise to a number of unhappy comparisons, even if it is untrue that, on hearing of it, the Kaiser ordered a special performance of "The Merry Wives of Saxe-Coburg and Gotha". More serious was the apparently deliberate attempt to keep the throne in the background during the conflict, though it is impossible to say whether this was due to the ministers, acting for their own ends, or to the timidity of some personal adviser of the King. At any rate Mr. Lloyd George's devotion to the cause of monarchy would appear to have left a good deal to be desired in view of his refusal to allow the Imperial Family of Russia to come to England after the Russian Revolution.

On the other hand, the war enabled all the members of the British Royal Family to come into personal contact with the mass of the people in a way and to an extent that had been unknown since the fall of the Stuarts. The King and Queen further set an example of duty which secured for them widespread respect, while the Prince of Wales laid the foundations of that personal popularity which was to be so marked during the years after the war. In the political and military field it would appear that the King only took the initiative on one occasion, but that was a most important one, and his action was decisive: he was undoubtedly the main factor in the removal of the then Sir John French from the command of the British troops on the Western Front, though he had the full support of Mr. Asquith. Nor was this all, for the coming of the First World War seems to have opened the King's eyes to more than one factor in the European situation which had previously escaped him. At any rate he is credited with observing to the Russian ambassador as early as September, 1914, that what mattered was not only the weakening of the power of Germany in Europe, but also that of the power of Prussia in the Reich, and with this end in view he advocated the revival of the kingdom of Hanover as one of the conditions of peace. Furthermore, he did what he could to further the negotiations instituted in the spring of 1917 by the Emperor Charles of Austria through his brother-in-law, Prince Sixte of Bourbon-Parma, and when revolution broke out in Central Europe the King took steps to ensure that the Austrian Emperor did not meet the fate of the Tsar.

In effect, then, whether or not the First World War strengthened the British monarchy as such, it undoubtedly enhanced the personal prestige of King George V and his eldest son.

Troubled as were the years which succeeded the signature of the Armistice in November, 1918, the Crown was not confronted with any such constitutional difficulties as had arisen at the beginning of the reign, though in the autumn of 1924 the King took a decision which caused a certain amount of comment, this time in Liberal quarters. The General Election of 1922 had given the Conservatives a majority of seventy, but in the following year another appeal to the country, necessitated by Mr. Baldwin's adoption of Tariff Reform, resulted in a House of Commons constituted as follows, 258 Conservatives, 191 Socialists, 159 Liberals, and 7 Independents. The Conservative Administration was defeated on the Address by the vote of the combined Liberal and Socialist parties, and was succeeded by the first Socialist Government under Mr. Ramsay MacDonald. A few months later the new ministry was in its turn defeated in the House of Commons, whereupon the Prime Minister asked the King for a dissolution which was at once granted him.

King George would have been perfectly within his rights had he refused this request, and called upon Mr. Asquith to form a government, which appears to have been the procedure which the Liberal leader had assumed would be adopted. He seems to have argued that in view of the fact there had been two General Elections in as many years the Sovereign would not permit another appeal to the country while there was still an alternative, that is to say a Liberal government with Conservative support. That Mr. Asquith had interpreted the working of the Constitution correctly is proved by the fact that in Canada two years later the Governor-General, Lord Byng, refused a like request of Mr. Mackenzie King in not dissimilar circumstances. King George, however, took a different course, and a General Election in the autumn of 1924 resulted in the return of a large Conservative majority.

The next few years, certain family considerations apart, were probably the least troubled that the King had known since he succeeded his father, and his popularity steadily grew throughout this period. How well he had laid the foundations of his hold upon the affections of his subjects was seen in November, 1928, when it was announced that he was seriously ill, and, in fact, for some weeks he hovered between life and death. The effect upon the country came as a surprise even to those who were most convinced of the monarchical instincts of the British people. Almost in a flash it became clear that the best-loved and most respected man in the Empire was its soveriegn, and every class of the community shared the anxiety of the Royal Family as the bulletins raised or lowered its hope. There had been nothing like it since the illness of the Prince of Wales over fifty years before, and for anything in the nature of an exact parallel one must go back to 1744 when Louis XV lay at death's door at Metz. The King had won not only the nation's confidence, but its love, by his unostentatious devotion to his duty and its interests, and in the difficult years which were so soon to follow it is this fact which may well have saved the throne.

While King George was recovering from his illness another crisis, not constitutional this time but political and economic, was approaching. One of the worst slumps in modern history was spreading across the world, while in Britain a General Election in the spring of 1929 returned the Socialists to the House of Commons as the strongest single party, but without an absolute majority, and Mr. MacDonald became Prime Minister dependent upon the support of a handful of Liberals led by Mr. Lloyd George. For two years the new Government struggled on amid rapidly increasing difficulties, of which a phenomenal rise in the number of unemployed was not the least, but by August, 1931, the brink of the abyss had been reached. The finances of the country were on the verge of collapse, and no satisfactory method of averting the impending catastrophe was even approximately acceptable to all three parties. It was the supreme moment in King George's life and reign, and, fortunately for his subjects, with twenty-one years' experience behind him he rose to the occasion.

He had only recently arrived at Balmoral from

Sandringham, fully aware of what was only too likely to happen, when he received, on August 22nd, a message from London to the effect that the Prime Minister would probably be asking him shortly to return to the capital. Without waiting for any such request the King decided at once to come South, and when his intention was known a sigh of relief went up from the whole country. His own views were perfectly clear. To quote Mr. John Gore in his *King George V:*

> It was for all hands to rally to the Captain to save the Ship of State from going to pieces on a lee shore. What he had heard of the political deadlock may have suggested to him that the existing Government ought to resign, that a National Government should take its place, and that in the complications of Party differences only Mr. MacDonald could lead that Government. But his own duty was clear, to hear all sides, to compose their differences as best he could, to counsel moderation and compromise, to invoke patriotism, and to encourage and re-inspire Mr. MacDonald by every means in his power.

In taking this line the King was unquestionably acting in accordance with the views of the man-in-the-street, and some very highly-coloured accounts were put in circulation of what took place during the various conferences that were held at Buckingham Palace with the party leaders. Of one thing there can be no doubt, and it is that the formation of the National Government was primarily the work of the King. There was no new group in or out of Parliament to which he could turn: he had to do his best with the existing political material. The sole alternative would have been to have called to power some national figure, if such a one could be found, but in view of the fact that no one was specially indicated it would have been a very dubious experiment.

At this point it may not be out of place to reflect upon what might have happened had Great Britain been a republic in August, 1931. The President would either have been a colourless nonentity or a violent partisan. If the former, he would never have dared to adopt a definite policy of his own, and at a time when every hour was of importance if catastrophe was to be avoided, days, and probably weeks, would have been wasted in consultations with the various party leaders before a new administration could have been formed. Had the President been a partisan he would not have possessed the confidence of the nation as a whole, and his chief concern would most likely have been, not the future of the country, but that of his political associates.

Professor Laski, in his pamphlet *The Crisis and the Constitution: 1931 and After*, has accused King George V of unconstitutional conduct, and in some circles the events of August, 1931, have been described as a palace revolution. The charge is that he should have accepted the resignation of the Socialist Government, and then sent for Mr. Baldwin to form a purely Conservative administration. On the other hand it can surely be argued much more convincingly that had the King not acted as he did he would have been violating the Constitution. He believed that the only hope of restoring the situation lay in the formation of a non-party government, and from the beginning he worked to this end. He could cite the recent precedent of over seven years of coalition administration in his support, while no one has ever questioned the right of the King of England to choose whom he will as Prime Minister. Custom has, in fact, generally narrowed his choice, but under the Constitution he has a perfectly free hand, and he was quite entitled to request Mr. MacDonald to form a national ministry on non-party lines. A British monarch would only be acting unconstitutionally if he kept in office an administration that could not obtain a majority in the House of Commons.

Finally, the government that was formed in August, 1931, carried all its measures by a sufficiency of votes, and when the General Election took place a few weeks later the electorate endorsed the monarch's action by an overwhelming majority. It was many a long year since a British sovereign had intervened so decisively in domestic politics, and the upshot was that King George V proved himself to be a shrewder judge both of the national interest and of his subjects' wishes than was a large part of his faithful Commons.

The King had little more than four years to live, and the most memorable event of that period was the Silver Jubilee of the reign in 1935. The idea of a Silver Jubilee would appear to have been a new one for nothing of that nature took place on the comparable dates of 1785 or 1862, but however this may be the reception accorded to the King and Queen was an eloquent testimony to the place which they and the monarchy held in the affections of the British people. Less than twelve months later, on January 20th, 1936, King George V died.

His death is too recent, and too much of the secret history of his reign is still of necessity undisclosed, for an exact estimate of the King to be yet attempted. Of one thing, however, there can be no question; there have been abler and more romantic Kings of England than King George V, but there has never been one with a greater sense of duty. It is arguable that he by no means always took the right course, but he certainly never acted from an unworthy motive. He lacked many of his father's virtues, as well as one or two of his weaknesses, but it may well be that when all the facts are known the verdict of history will be that the British monarchy escaped the fate of so many thrones elsewhere owing to the personal character of King George V.

V

THE LATEST REIGNS

A Latent Crisis—King George V and the Prince of Wales—The Upbringing of King Edward VIII—His Popularity—Breakers Ahead—The Abdication—Mr. Baldwin's Skill—State of Public Opinion—Attitude of the Archbishop of Canterbury—Difficulties of King George VI—His Happy Marriage—Position of the Crown To-Day—Accession of Queen Elizabeth II—Neglect of Leaders of Thought—Obsolete Social Conventions— The Royal Family and Foreign Royalty—The Appeal of the Throne

THE CRISIS which it was now destined that the monarchy should undergo had been latent during the last years of King George V, though it was only patent to a small circle in the Court and political world of the capital. Indeed, in retrospect it is impossible not to reflect with some degree of surprise upon the ignorance of even otherwise well-informed people concerning what was at issue until the Bishop of Bradford made his now famous pronouncement. Abroad, the position of the new King was freely discussed both in public and in private, but few people in England read foreign newspapers, and the British Press left the subject severely alone.

The background was the long dynastic tradition of friction between the reigning monarch and the heir-apparent, to which the only exception had been the happy relations which existed between King Edward VII and the Prince of Wales of those days. At the same time it must be borne in mind that the future King George V had a respect for his father that almost amounted to reverence, and if he was not altogether blind to the older man's few weaknesses he was certainly deaf to any mention of them. In these circumstances it would not be wholly surprising if King George, given his upbringing in an atmosphere of naval discipline, looked for a similar attitude on the part of his eldest son. In effect, the departure from the tradition of over two hundred years had only been possible because from 1901 to 1910 the Prince of Wales had been in affectionate awe of his father. There was no guarantee, or even likelihood, that this condition would be repeated in the next reign, nor did such prove to be the case.

From the beginning there was clearly a fundamental difference of outlook between King George V and the Prince of Wales, and in the difficulties which in consequence ensued between them is to be found the clue to the abdication. Had their relations been happier, much of what was to take place might never have occurred, for the Prince would have looked to his own family for comfort and support. The time has not yet come to consider the part played by those hereditary strains of Guelph and Coburg ancestry to which allusion has been made on an earlier page, but they, too, must have counted for a great deal.

The training of King Edward VIII had been very different from that of his father. In the first place he had from his earliest days been brought up as heir to the throne, and he was not yet twenty-one when he was thrown into the turmoil of the First World War. Such an upbringing bore little resemblance to the strict Service career of his father while he was still Duke of York. Then, when the war was over, and his contemporaries were settling down to a normal peacetime existence, were marrying and being given in marriage, he was for long away from England on those tours of the overseas Empire which, in conjunction with the broadcasts of King George V, did so much to make the throne a living thing at the very ends of the earth. In these circumstances it is small wonder that he grew restless, and, it must be confessed, out of touch and patience with much that his parents and their generation still held dear.

What is remarkable is not that there should have been sharp differences between father and son, but that the public estrangements of their ancestors should have been avoided. There was nothing approaching even the occasional scandals that marked the relations of the Regent and his daughter. In some of his writings since the abdication the Duke of Windsor has borne testimony to the very great affection which he entertained for his grandfather, King Edward VII, and this prompts a regret that King Edward did not live a few years longer so as to have had the supervision of the upbringing of his grandson. The devotion of the young man to the old one was clearly there, and the tact and experience of King Edward VII might well have corrected several tendencies which the more direct, but less skilful, methods of King George V failed to alter. There is no one from whom a young man is more likely to take advice than from a kindly man-of-the-world, which King Edward VII certainly was, and King George V as certainly was not.

Furthermore, by the time that King Edward VIII came to the throne he had achieved a degree of popularity which no other Prince of Wales had ever known. Stories to his disadvantage, chiefly in respect of his manners, were, it is true, going round the West End clubs, but they were either unknown to, or not believed by, the mass of the population. On the other hand there could be no question of the sincerity of his interest in social reform, or of his desire to alleviate the existing widespread unemployment, and the last public act of his short reign was a visit to the distressed areas of South Wales, where the warmth of his reception testified to the hold which he had at any rate over the less fortunate of his subjects. Had the crisis come over almost any other subject than that which was its cause, and had the King stood his ground, a royal *coup d'état* would have enjoyed such support as to have rendered resistance hopeless, for all the majority which Mr. Baldwin had obtained at the General Election of the previous year.

Much has been written about the abdication of King Edward VIII in December, 1936, and doubtless more will be written in the future, though whether there will prove to be anything fresh to say is another matter. What has to be avoided in this connection is the temptation to read history backwards. Because the crisis of that time was successfully surmounted this does not mean that it might not have had an entirely different outcome, or that it did not shake the throne to its very foundations. Those who can carry their memories back to the particular week when the crisis actually broke will testify that people, whatever their walk of life, spoke and thought of nothing else, and it was well said that Hitler might have seized Austria without the British public either knowing or caring. It was, indeed, a unique experience in the national history.

The crisis was the more acute because it was, at any rate for the overwhelming mass of the people, entirely unexpected. It is true that even before the death of King George V the partiality of the Heir Apparent for Mrs. Simpson had become obvious to a few persons in Court and political circles, but these circles were exceedingly small. This partiality became more widely known as the year 1936 advanced, but in retrospect what is surprising is not how many, but how few, people were aware of the direction in which events were moving. Not a word was allowed to appear in the Press, though whether this silence was for the good either of the King or of his subjects is a moot point. There were, of course, references in plenty in the American and Continental papers, but they are not widely read in England, and so the news did not spread very far. The very unexpectedness of the crisis resulted in a general confusion as to what was at stake, and this in its turn led to somewhat wild fluctuations in public opinion and public sympathy.

All the relevant information will clearly not be available until the principal actors in the drama, as it may without exaggeration be termed, have passed away, but the main facts do not admit of serious question. Before 1936 was far advanced, though the actual date is not fully established, the Cabinet became aware that sooner or later the King would express his wish to marry Mrs. Simpson, and that as she had been through the divorce-court this would give rise to every kind of complication. In the first place there was, in view of the teaching of the Church of England on the whole question of divorce, the question whether the Archbishop of Canterbury could or would crown a man who was married to a divorced woman; let alone whether he would crown, should the eventuality arise, the woman herself. Then there was the attitude of the Empire overseas to be considered, and upon this there was no reliable information. At no time, it may be added, does there appear to have been any official objection entertained towards Mrs. Simpson on the ground that she was a commoner or an American. Indeed, no objection could have been raised on the first score in view of the fact that the Heir Presumptive, the Duke of York, had himself married a commoner.

The first interview between the King and the Prime Minister, Mr. Stanley Baldwin, took place on October 20th. In recalling the interviews which he had on this day and on others that followed, Mr. Baldwin spoke of the King's manner. "Never has he shown any sign of offence, of being hurt at anything I have said to him. The whole of our discussions have been carried out, as I have said, with an increase, if possible, of that mutual respect and regard in which we stood". Mr. Baldwin explained to the King his anxiety concerning the rumours which were reaching him, and at the end of their talk the Sovereign observed, "You and I must settle this matter together; I will not have anyone interfering". It was a month before the two men met again.

Public allusion to the matter was made by the Bishop of Bradford on December 1st, and from that moment an early settlement was essential. At the end of November the King first declared his intention to abdicate and marry as a private citizen, but then he expressed a desire to make a morganatic marriage. Mr. Neville Chamberlain, then Chancellor of the Exchequer, noted in his diary, "I have no doubt that if it were possible to arrange the morganatic marriage, this would only be the prelude to the further step, of making Mrs. Simpson Queen with full rights". Mr. Chamberlain's views were those of his colleagues, and on December 2nd the Cabinet unanimously agreed they could not be responsible for the legislation which a morganatic marriage would require. To quote Mr. Keith Feiling's *Life of Neville Chamberlain*, "Their position was dangerous, for everything in human nature, from pure metal to base clay, was now engaged. With their curious complex of sensation, political cowardice, and thirst for power, the cheap press were taking a hand; they must reckon with the loyalties of Churchill, and the political possibilities of a clash between sovereign and Cabinet. Many had justly seen in King Edward qualities for the making of a great sovereign; why, it was put to democracy, should he not marry the woman of his choice? Why put a pistol to the head of this lonely man for an instant decision? So the legend grew, and danger with it".

In the handling of this situation the Prime Minister showed remarkable skill, and during his three Premierships nothing became him better. This was the more surprising to contemporaries because when the crisis broke his personal prestige had reached its nadir owing to the way in which he had mishandled the Hoare-Laval Pact twelve months earlier. It was largely due to him that the relevant proceedings in the House of Commons were dignified, though in the line he took Mr. Baldwin was fortunately able to rely upon the support of Mr. Attlee, then Leader of the Opposition. Tribute must also be paid to King Edward himself, for his decision to remain at Fort Belvedere prevented those public demonstrations which would undoubtedly have occurred had he returned to London, and which might so easily have developed into serious rioting.

In effect, from first to last there were only three solutions: the first was the King's marriage, with Mrs. Simpson as Queen; the second was abdication and marriage; and the third was renunciation of this particular marriage altogether. The first of these was soon barred, because apart altogether from feeling in Great Britain itself the Dominions had declared against it. The choice thus lay between the second and third courses, and it was the third which his subjects wished the King would adopt. He thought otherwise and abdicated, so that on December 11th, 1936, his brother, the Duke of York, ascended the throne as King George VI. For the first time since 1483 the country had known three monarchs in the same year.

One man was, and in many quarters still is, considered to have come very badly out of the crisis, and that is the then Archbishop of Canterbury, Cosmo Lang. It would be foolish to deny that in consequence the Church of England suffered some damage. Mr. J. G. Lockhart, in his biography of Archbishop Lang, has clearly proved that the Primate played no part in the negotiations leading up to the abdication, contrary to the opinion of contemporaries. Where the Archbishop did lay himself open to criticism was in the line he took in his broadcast, where he spoke of King Edward having "disappointed hopes so high", and abandoning "a trust so great". This gave the impression that he was "kicking a man who was down"; such an attitude never appeals to the British public, and it is especially repellent in a Christian priest. When much else concerning the abdication has been forgotten, this unhappy broadcast is likely to be remembered.

It has already been suggested that because this crisis was not of long duration, and because it was skilfully handled, there are no grounds for the assumption that it was not of the utmost gravity. In slightly different circumstances the position of the monarchy might have become so insecure as to bring the throne to the ground. The late Sir Arnold Wilson, M.P., for example, gave it as his opinion that if a straight vote of the House of Commons had been taken not less than a hundred votes would have been cast in favour of the establishment of a republic.

Such was the abdication crisis, which would undoubtedly have figured more prominently in British history had it not been so soon overshadowed by the outbreak of the Second World War. In a country with so long a record as Great Britain it is rare to come across any constitutional event which can accurately be described as unparalleled, yet that epithet can definitely be applied to the abdication of King Edward VIII. It is true that since the Norman Conquest several English monarchs have died otherwise than in possession of their regal functions, but this has been due to pressure from outside rather than to their own wish. Edward II and Richard II may technically have abdicated, but in fact they were deposed; certainly no English sovereign had renounced the throne when not only were other courses open to him, but were actually being urged upon him by his ministers.

It was this particular aspect of the crisis which came as the greatest shock to the ordinary citizen, and particularly to those who were of King Edward's own generation. Much water, and not a little blood, has flowed under the bridges since those December days of 1936, and there is no more desire now than there was then to be censorious, but the voluntary abdication seemed, and still seems, a sad end to the high hopes that had so long been entertained. As Mr. Hector Bolitho has written, "The King's life had been a pathway of promises from the day when he walked in Caernarvon Castle to vow to his father that he would always be a "husband" to his people. These pledges were recalled during the early days of the last week of his reign. Business men in Manchester were able to remember the day when he leaned across a table and said, 'I shall always pull my weight'. Even the dusky Maoris in New Zealand were able to think of the day when he said to them, 'I will ever keep before me the pattern of Victoria, the Great Queen'. In almost every land of the earth, over a period of twenty years, he had frowned, with the earnestness which had always made his utterances attractive, and had promised that his heart and his talents belonged to the people. It did not seem possible that he would turn from this good history to embrace the smaller needs of his heart".

The succeeding monarch, King George VI, thus came to the throne in circumstances of exceptional difficulty. It is true that his father, too, had not been Heir Apparent in his earlier years, but in spite of this King George V had afterwards served a considerable apprenticeship as Prince of Wales: his second son, on the contrary, was called most unexpectedly to the throne, almost at a moment's notice. Nor was this all, for the basis of the monarchy had been seriously shaken, and there was much harm to be undone. Finally, the times were far from normal, and the shadow of the Third Reich was falling across the whole world.

In the years of his youth the new King was probably less concerned than any of his brothers in the attending of public functions in an official capacity or as a representative of Royalty. His early training had been that of a professional sailor, for he had passed through Osborne and Dartmouth. During the First World War he served in *Collingwood* at the battle of Jutland, and for his coolness and courage under fire was mentioned in despatches. During the years of peace which followed he began to carry out various public engagements, though it was not until June, 1920, that he was created Duke of York. He represented King George V at the formal entry of the King of the Belgians into Brussels in November, 1918; he paid visits to Jugoslavia and Rumania; and, after his marriage, he paid state visits to Africa and Australasia. These activities were naturally recalled with respect by his new subjects, to whom, it must be confessed, the King was not very well known at his accession.

Throughout his life he had been overshadowed by his elder brother, and he had been content that this should be the case.

There were, however, two considerations which made for popularity; one was his work in connection with "The Duke of York's Camp", and the other was his marriage to Lady Elizabeth Bowes-Lyon.

"The Duke of York's Camp" was organized under the auspices of the Industrial Welfare Society, and it was first held at New Romney in 1921, after which it became an annual event. Boys from each of a hundred schools and boys from a hundred firms were invited each year as the Duke's guests to the camp, and between the inauguration of the scheme and the King's accession nearly six thousand boys passed through the camp. During this period there was only one occasion when, through illness, the King missed visiting the camp, where he invariably took part in all its activities. One story will illustrate his keen participation in what went on. A game of push-ball was in prospect, and it was suggested that the future King should referee. "Referee be blowed", came the reply, "I am going to play", and play he did. In the middle of the game, when both sides had their heads hard down to it, a young Rugger Blue was boring with his head into the ribs of a player in front of him. Giving him a tremendous butt, he shouted, "Go on, push like the devil!" In a flash, the Duke of York's voice came out of the *mêlée*, "But I am pushing like the devil". It was the royal ribs that had been butted so generously.

The Duke's marriage with Lady Elizabeth Bowes-Lyon had taken place at Westminster Abbey in April, 1923, and formalities which preceeded it are an interesting commentary upon the history of the British Royal Family. At a special meeting of the

Privy Council in the previous February, in pursuance of the Royal Marriage Act of 1772, a document was signed signifying the royal assent "to the contracting of matrimony between His Royal Highness Albert Frederick Arthur George, Duke of York, and the Lady Elizabeth Angela Margaret Bowes-Lyon, youngest daughter of the Right Honourable Claude George, Earl of Strathmore and Kinghorne". This procedure was rendered necessary, as indicated above, by the Royal Marriage Act which declared that "No descendant of George II (other than the issue of princesses married or who may marry into foreign families) shall be capable of contracting matrimony without the previous consent of the King, signified under the Great Seal, declared in Council and entered in the Privy Council books". This act had been passed at the insistence of George III because two of his brothers had contracted marriages with women not of the Blood Royal, and to whom he personally objected on social and political grounds.

In marrying a commoner, the Duke of York was breaking an old precedent. Queen Victoria, it is true, had allowed one of her daughters to marry the Marquess of Lorne, afterwards Duke of Argyll, and a sister of King George V had married the Duke of Fife, but it was two and half centuries since a prince in direct succession to the throne had wedded a commoner. Curiously enough, that prince was also a sailor, namely James, Duke of York, afterwards King James II, and his bride was Anne Hyde, daughter of the Earl of Clarendon. This return to the customs of a more generous age was universally popular, and it marked the beginning of that hold upon the nation's affections which has been so marked a feature of the career of the present Queen Mother.

It is impossible to regard objectively the reign of a

monarch recently dead, for the relevant information on such important matters as his relations with his ministers is necessarily lacking. These considerations apply with special force to the reign of King George VI, but one or two reflections upon that reign may, perhaps, be permitted.

In his first message to Parliament, and through it to all his subjects, the new King said:

> I have succeeded to the throne in circumstances which are without precedent and at a moment of great personal distress; but I am resolved to do my duty, and I am sustained by the knowledge that I am supported by the widespread goodwill and sympathy of all my subjects here and throughout the world.
>
> It will be my constant endeavour, with God's help, supported as I shall be by my dear wife, to uphold the honour of the realm and promote the happiness of my peoples.

This struck what was to be the keynote of the reign, namely character, and the reputation which he early acquired for this stood the King in excellent stead in the difficult years of the Second World War and its aftermath.

It must, however, be admitted that it is by no means easy for the monarchy to play its rightful part in the national life while a section of the press is continually, though in most cases quite unintentionally, making it ridiculous. Does a member of the Royal Family relax for a moment, then his or her photograph at that moment is reproduced in the papers of the following day for the delectation of millions. The camera has imposed fresh responsibilities upon all who are in public life, but particularly upon Royalty. The elaborate ceremonial with which Louis XIV passed through life was not organized by him merely to gratify his own vanity, but because he realized that the divinity which hedges Kings must have its outward and visible sign, and this purpose is hardly served by pictures of princesses in bathing attire, or of princes in their shirt-sleeves.

The direct political influence of the popular press in Great Britain to-day is probably not extensive, but its power of suggestion is enormous. For this reason it is highly undesirable that matters relating to Royalty should be discussed in that jocular vein which is peculiar to a certain type of British journalism; such a tone may be venial in the United States, which is a republic, but it is quite out of place in Great Britain, and it is surprising to find it employed in the columns of papers that call themselves Conservative. It is true that the British Royal Family itself is rarely subjected to treatment of this sort, though headline references to Princess Margaret as "Margaret" leave a good deal to be desired in the matter of taste, but its foreign relatives are often held up to ridicule. "Exclusive" stories professing to relate the inside history of this or that foreign Court are by no means uncommon, and the reader is familiarized with the members of Imperial and Royal Families under such nicknames as "Little Willie" and "Foxy" Ferdinand.

In reality, the private lives of Presidents and business-men, even of newspaper proprietors themselves, are often far more lurid than those of Royalty, for few princes can show such a record as Ivar Kreuger, or have met their death in the interesting circumstances that marked the demise of Félix Faure. Yet they have not the attraction for the newspaper-reader of a scandal in which Royalty is involved, for the simple reason that the story of a monarch's shortcomings makes a subtle appeal to the inferiority complex. From the point of view of circulation, therefore, there is much to be said for treating Royalty in a manner which has become only too common, but in view of the Communist cloud upon the horizon of European civilization the press magnate who allows his editors to print this type of article is merely sawing through the branch upon which he himself is sitting.

It has already been remarked that the position of the future King George VI was greatly strengthened by his marriage, and it would be impossible to over-emphasize the asset which the present Queen Mother has been to the British monarchy. With all his solid virtues the late King's approach to strangers was somewhat hesitant, and his Queen was singularly successful in eradicating any unfortunate impressions to which this weakness might from time to time give rise. Queen Mary, too, in old age proved to be a pillar of strength, and, as in the case of Queen Victoria, an earlier unpopularity was completely forgotten. Indeed the late King was both lucky in, and was supported by, his immediate relatives, which is a great deal more than can be said for many of his predecessors on the throne. On the other hand, all the evidence goes to show that the death of the Duke of Kent, coming when it did, was a real misfortune, not least because the dead prince moved in those literary and artistic circles with which the other members of the Royal Family are not very closely in touch.

Circumstances, of which in the last years of his life illness played an unhappy part, circumscribed the King's activities outside the British Isles, for unsettled conditions rendered it impossible for him to go to some of the countries which he would normally have visited. In spite of this he and the Queen went to Canada and South Africa, and, abroad, to France and the United States, while foreign monarchs and presidents received hospitality at Buckingham Palace. The lot of King George VI, however, did not fall in such spacious days as that of his grandfather, and in the main the influence of the monarchy was felt much nearer home. Particularly was this the case during the Second World War, and when the Luftwaffe bombed Buckingham Palace if forged new links between the Royal Family and the people of Britain; how strong these links were was shown in the evident grief of the citizens of London when the King died. The great contribution which the throne made to the national life during the reign was to provide a symbol of stability and continuity in a revolutionary age, and just the right impression was made by the spectacle of its occupant doing his duty quietly and unostentatiously. On all sides there was a deplorable lack of unity; everywhere the politicians were stressing what keeps men apart rather than what brings them together, but King George VI saw to it that the Crown was at once the emblem and the hope of a more sane state of affairs.

Nor is this all, for the monarchy provides that element of colour and romance for which mankind craves, and which is rapidly vanishing from the drab democratic world of modern times. The enormous crowds which every year flock to the Birthday Parade are proof of this. This great concourse of people does not come to see a display of armed might, and it is certainly not inspired by any spirit of jingoism. The London public turns out in its tens of thousands to see a great British tradition worthily maintained. Forty years ago a ceremony along similar lines could have been seen in any of the large European capitals, but to-day such pageantry is hardly even a memory except in London. The ordinary citizen looks on the Birthday Parade as a link with the past, and whatever his political opinions he rarely wants to break such links, nor is the plight of those nations which have done so any great encouragement to him to follow their example. "The councils to which Time is not called", wrote Sir Walter Raleigh, "Time will not ratify". In this mechanical and materialistic age the Birthday Parade is a reminder of what Time represents in the life of a nation, and it impresses upon the least imaginative the fact that English history did not begin yesterday.

On the other hand nothing but harm to the monarchy can result from the attempt of any political party to use it for the furtherance of a sectional interest, as the course of events in Northern Ireland clearly proves. In this connection it is significant that the last royal visit to the Union of South Africa was followed by the defeat of Field-Marshal Smuts at the polls, and it may well be that this was in some measure due to resentment at the extent to which he had attempted during the visit to identify the throne with his own party. If such was the case then it is a great tribute to the statesmanship of Dr. Malan that he should once more have taken the Crown out of South African politics by inviting King George VI to spend a holiday in the Union. Unhappily that visit was destined never to take place, but the fact that the invitation was given and accepted must go a long way towards the goal for which the monarch and the statesman alike were striving.

When all is said and done the strength of the British monarchy to-day is due to the conviction of the ordinary citizen that the occupant of the throne has "no axe to grind", and King George VI fortified this belief by his example. There is no such belief in the disinterestedness of any politician, whatever his party; and what is true of Great Britain is even more true of the white Dominions. The exact constitutional position of the British Commonwealth of Nations at the present time is not easy to determine, but there can be little doubt that it is largely held together by the common Crown. That the monarchy is able to perform this service is not the least of the accomplishments of recent Sovereigns.

Four British monarchs have died during the course of the present century, but there is a marked difference between the three earlier deaths and the demise of King George VI. Queen Victoria was an old woman, and it was not to be expected that she would live much longer. The death of King Edward VII was relatively sudden, but, even so, sufficient time elapsed for the public to be prepared for the worst. In the case of King George V, he was sinking for several days before he died, and there was never any real hope that he would recover. By contrast, it was the tragic suddenness of the late King's death, just at the time when the man in the street believed that he was well on the way to recovery, that shocked, as well as moved, the public. What history will say of King George VI remains to be seen, but of one thing there can surely be no doubt—he left the monarchy a great deal stronger than he found it.

Great Britain now has a new Queen, and it is indeed well that she should, like Elizabeth I and Victoria, have come to the throne in all the freshness and vigour of youth. In these circumstances it is not unimportant to consider certain aspects of the relations between the monarchy and the country at what may prove to be the beginning of a new era in their history, for it would be idle to pretend that everything is perfect where the throne is concerned.

It is, for instance, to be hoped that in the new reign efforts will be made to bring the Crown into closer touch with the leaders of thought. This is not to say members of the Royal Family have up to now refrained from giving their patronage to the arts, but they do not come into personal and unofficial contact with men of letters to anything like the extent that they do with politicians, generals, admirals, and captains of industry. This neglect of those who are moulding the opinion of the rising generation is a serious, if common, mistake on the part of monarchs, and it has had much to do with the disasters that have overtaken some of them. It is true that in England a man of letters counts for less than in any other country in the world, but he is not wholly insignificant. It is really not enough for the Presidents of the various Royal Societies to be invited to a garden party at Buckingham Palace once a year.

As has been shown on an earlier page, King Edward VII finally broke the Victorian prejudice against "trade", and invited in large numbers those who were engaged in industry and commerce, first of all to Marlborough House, when he was Prince of Wales, and afterwards to Buckingham Palace. In this way he frustrated any tendency on the part of the *haute bourgeoisie* to become anti-monarchical, as happened in Russia, where they actually supplied the Bolshevists with money to overturn the Tsar, who had ignored them. What seems to be required now is that the monarchy should associate itself with the thought of the country in the same way that King Edward VII associated it with commercial and industrial activity. There is real danger in a situation where a man of letters does not come into intimate contact with Royalty unless he happens to possess some social or political qualification such as a title or membership of the legislature. Of all the activities of the country at the present time the Royal Family is probably most ignorant of the intellectual.

It is also by no means improbable that Queen Elizabeth II will find much to remedy in the matter of the presentation of debutantes and similar ceremonial functions. For example, the pageantry that is associated with Ascot is admirable, but its significance is diminished by the fact that while admission to the Royal Enclosure, which is Her Majesty's private lawn, is only possible upon the production of tickets issued by the Lord Chamberlain, these tickets have to be paid for, and they are by no means cheap.

At the same time there is certainly no desire on the part of the British people to see the Court come to resemble that of the July Monarchy or of the Second Empire in France, when the provincial *bourgeoisie* and the shady financier were the chosen companions of Royalty. Indeed, if ever times improve, there are several of the old functions that might well be revived, for pageantry is dear to the hearts of the British, who do not even mind paying for it. What is essential for the Royal Family is to avoid at all costs the impression that access to it depends upon wealth. In Great Britain there is a widespread respect for birth, and of late years even a tolerance for the possession of brains, but for mere money there is, outside the so-called "smart set", no reverence at all. Money gets what it will purchase, but nothing more, and it would be an evil day for the monarchy were there ever to be a suspicion that upon the size of a man's bank account depended his reception at Buckingham Palace.

It would also be dangerous for the British monarchy were every other state in Europe, save Great Britain, to become a republic, and of late years sight has been lost of that international monarchist solidarity upon which both Queen Victoria and King Edward VII laid so much stress. All regimes derive strength or weakness from the success or failure of those of a similar nature elsewhere, and a monarchy is no exception. One of the outstanding monarchical triumphs since the Second World War has been achieved in Greece, yet when Prince Philip of that country was about to marry the then Princess Elizabeth the most elaborate procedure was adopted to conceal from the British public that fact that he was a member of the Greek Royal Family. This is the more extraordinary because, in view of its Danish origin, the Greek dynasty is one of the oldest in Europe—compared with it the Mountbattens are of yesterday—while the Greeks themselves were the loyal allies of Great Britain against Hitler and Mussolini. Whoever was responsible for this particular asininity had little knowledge of history or the British character, and still less respect for the monarchical principle.

PART TWO
MONARCHY ABROAD

I

THE SPANISH MONARCHY

The Inheritance of King Alfonso XIII—Breakdown of Parliamentary Government—The Moroccan Disaster—Formation of the Military Directory—King Alfonso and General Primo de Rivera—Strength and Weakness of the Military Directory—Its Fall—Alternatives before the King—The Hesitations of General Berenguer—The Gathering Storm—Results of the Local Elections—Collapse of the Monarchy—Some Reasons for Its Fall—Prospects of a Return of the Bourbons—Attitude of the Traditionalists—Don Juan and General Franco—A Monarchy without a Monarch

THE COLLAPSE of the Spanish monarchy in April, 1931, undoubtedly took the world by surprise, and it is generally believed that not one of the ambassadors at Madrid had warned his government that there was any serious prospect of revolution. For centuries Spain has had a by no means undeserved reputation as a country where the expected never, and the unexpected usually, happens, and its recent annals have certainly afforded ground for this charge. King Alfonso XIII had survived so many crises that there seemed to be no reason why he should ever be unseated, while the First Republic had, within living memory, been such a failure that a second essay in republicanism appeared unlikely to recommend itself to the Spanish people. So argued the foreign observer, thinking in terms of the other countries of western and central Europe; but the event proved him wrong, and it was typical of Spain that when, for the third time in little more than a century, the House of Bourbon was compelled to go into exile, it should be as the result of local elections in which the monarchists obtained an overwhelming majority.

In 1868 there had been a revolution which in its essence was a forecast of that of 1931. A small minority drove the Bourbons from the throne, and Isabella II, like her grandson on the later occasion, preferred to go into exile rather than to light the fires of civil war. For two years the crown was, literally, hawked round Europe, and, as in the previous century, the question of the Spanish succession resulted in an outbreak of hostilities, in this instance between France and Germany. Eventually an Italian prince, Amadeo of Savoy, was called to the throne, which he occupied uneasily for a brief space, and then abdicated. The First Republic followed, and in view of its record it is impossible to feel surprise at the misrule that was to be so prominent a feature of its successor. The Carlists (as the followers of the legitimist claimant, Don Carlos, were called) at once declared war on the regime, and several provinces passed out of the control of the Madrid government. There were three Presidents within a year, and each of them represented a different form of republic. The Spanish fleet was seized by the extremists, and to prevent it embarking upon a piratical career in the Mediterranean it was interned at Gibraltar by the British authorities. The credit of Spain abroad reflected the chaos at home. On December 31st, 1873, the 3 per cent Exterior Debt was quoted on the London Stock Exchange at $17\frac{1}{4}$, and the coupons on this issue remained unpaid for eighteen months, having to be refunded later by the government of the Restoration.

In these circumstances the *pronunciamiento* of General Martinez Campos in favour of Isabella's son, Alfonso XII, met with widespread support, and in 1875 he ascended the throne of his ancestors. Although the

movement for the restoration of the monarchy was thus
military in its origin, the foremost statesman was a
civilian, Antonio Cánovas del Castillo, and it was he
who set Spain upon the course which she followed for a
generation. The constitution which was adopted at his
suggestion was modelled upon that of Great Britain,
though the administration of the country continued to
be along those French lines which had been established
in the previous century. In reality, the whole affair
was an elaborate sham. There were, it is true, two
parties, a Conservative and a Liberal, led by Cánovas
and Sagasta respectively, but the elections were
notoriously "made" so that a Conservative and a
Liberal majority should alternate. By far the greater
part of the electors were illiterate, and political power
resided in the *cacique*, or local "boss". At the same time,
it would be quite unfair to blame Cánovas for his
action. The King's title was not a good one, and the
staunchest monarchists were the followers of Don
Carlos. Moreover, he hoped that in due course the
constitution would take firm root, and as he had given
both the Crown and the Church a considerable part in
it he had some grounds for believing that in the long
run it might prove not unsuited to the national genius.

For some years there was every reason to suppose
that this hope would be justified. Spain survived
without any serious threat of disturbance the
premature death of Alfonso XII in 1885, and the long
minority of his posthumous son, which included the
disastrous war with the United States. Materially, too,
she prospered, but the constitution continued to be a
farce. So long as Cánovas and Sagasta lived the
outward appearances of the Parliamentary System
were decently preserved, but when they died the
parties which they had led began to break up into
groups. Canalejas possibly, and Dato certainly, might

have infused fresh life into the constitution, but of the numerous other Prime Ministers during this period those who were not corrupt were incompetent, and many were both. The age-old centrifugal tendencies once more began to make themselves felt, and the political life of the country degenerated into the internecine strife of the various groups, engendered by the jealousies of their respective leaders. To make matters worse, there were revolutionary strikes in all parts of the country, and in 1909 there took place in Barcelona disturbances that for a time seemed to herald another essay in republicanism. "My guns were in the pockets of the ministers", Admiral Cervera is reported to have observed to his American captors, and the remark well illustrates the corrupt conditions of Spanish public life at the time it was uttered.

Such being the case, King Alfonso found himself compelled more and more to take the exercise of power into his own hands. For days at a time there was no ministry, and when decisions had to be made the monarch was the only person who could make them. On the other hand, he had no capable advisers, and although material progress was considerable, Spain was still very poor, and physically she was exhausted after her efforts in the sixteenth and seventeenth centuries. She had thrown herself into the colonization of the New World with all the ardour of procreation, and the reaction was inevitable. A fog of pessimism, which not even the activity of the young King could disperse, settled down upon the country, and Spain became, in foreign eyes, the synonym for a nation that had had its day.

The First World War transformed Spain. It brought her riches which she had not known since the wealth of the Indies had been poured into her lap in the days of the *conquistadores*, and whole districts were industrialized almost overnight to supply the demands of the Allies. Stock of all kinds attained prices never known before, and as Spain resolutely adhered to her neutrality she reaped the maximum benefit from the conflict. At the same time, this wave of prosperity increased the growing dissatisfaction with the governmental machine, for the politicians proved quite incapable of taking advantage of what was happening to initiate a real national revival. They continued to play the old wearisome game of "ins" and "outs" with never a thought to the chance they were missing of setting Spain on her feet again for all time. As the leading neutral, she should have played a very prominent part indeed both in the peace settlement and in the post-war era, and that she did not do so, save during the tenure of office of General Primo de Rivera, was due to her political leaders.

The one Spaniard who enhanced his country's reputation during these critical years was the King. The work which he did at his own personal expense on behalf of the prisoners-of-war is in itself sufficient to counterbalance all the charges that his enemies have brought against him on other counts. For this purpose he maintained a secretariat of forty clerks, and the cost of postage alone was over a million pesetas. Nor was this by any means all, for King Alfonso exerted both diplomatic and personal pressure for the relief of suffering humanity. His initiative led to the cessation of reprisals in Germany against French prisoners; he took up strongly the case of the civil population of Lille; and he never ceased to protest against the horrors of unrestricted submarine warfare. Eight sentences of death on women, and twenty on men, were commuted in consequence of his intervention, while had the Marqués de Villalobar, the Spanish minister at Brussels, had time to communicate with

Madrid, Edith Cavell would assuredly not have been shot. These things should be remembered now when many of those on whose behalf King Alfonso toiled are so ready to denigrate his memory, though the reception which was accorded to him both in Paris and London after the Spanish Revolution in 1931 is evidence that the people of France and England had not forgotten the part he had played. The fact was that King Alfonso, like his relatives the Emperors Francis Joseph and Charles of Austria, regarded war in the old chivalrous spirit.

Hardly had the First World War come to an end than the Moroccan question in an acute form came to occupy Spanish attention, and some account of it is essential in view of the charges subsequently brought against King Alfonso in this connection. Ever since the middle of the nineteenth century the affairs of the Shereefian Empire had been closely followed in the Peninsula, and for France and Spain the Moorish kingdom presented much the same problem as the future of Turkey had raised for Russia and Austria at the other end of the Mediterranean. In the early years of the present century events began to move rapidly. In concluding the Entente with France the British Government renounced interest in Morocco, and, as a result of the Algeciras Conference of 1906, France and Spain were given a free hand in that country. The increasing weakness of the Sultan's administration a few years later resulted in the two Powers dividing Morocco into zones of influence, and, within her sphere, Spain began the task of civilization. In July, 1921, this work was rudely interrupted by the surprise and annihilation at Anual of the army of General Silvestre by the Moors under Abd-el-Krim. Not only was this one of the worst disasters which until that date European troops had sustained at the hands of natives, and not only did the Spaniards lose at a blow all that had been gained by fourteen years of strenuous warfare, but subsequent investigation showed that successive governments had ignored the advice of their advisers, and that, if the immediate cause of the catastrophe was the temerity of General Silvestre, the real responsibility lay with the politicians in Madrid.

So long as King Alfonso lived he was accused by opponents of the monarchy of being responsible for the Anual disaster. It was alleged that he ordered General Silvestre to advance more rapidly than the military situation warranted, and unknown to the Minister for War and the High Commissioner in Morocco. No evidence, however, has been brought forward in support of this allegation, although during the lifetime of the Second Republic those who made it had the State archives at their disposal. The truth is that Silvestre was a rash and impetuous commander, who certainly needed no prompting to plunge into the mountains of the Riff without adequate preparation. The accusation against King Alfonso was really part of a campaign to calumniate the monarchy, and the attempt to implicate him in the overthrow of Silvestre had as much foundation in fact as would a similar effort to hold Queen Victoria responsible for the death of Gordon, or King George V for the surrender of Kut.

Anual brought to a head the discontent that had long been growing in the Peninsula, and as the only Parliamentarian of any ability, namely the afore-mentioned Dato, had been murdered earlier in the year it was obvious that a violent change of some sort was inevitable ere long. In addition to the strain of the Moroccan campaign Spain was suffering from internal disorders of the most serious nature. All the native anarchy of the race came to the surface, and revolutionary strikes, accompanied by bloodshed, were everywhere the order of the day. Communist emissaries would appear at a factory, and compel the men employed there to cease work without assigning any reason for their action, and such was the terror they inspired that they were rarely disobeyed. Murders were perpetrated with impunity, and even on the rare occasions when the criminals were caught, the jurors invariably acquitted them out of fear of the consequence to themselves of a conviction. In June, 1923, the disorders reached their climax in the assassination of the Cardinal Archbishop of Zaragoza, and on September 13th of the same year General Primo de Rivera made a *prounciamiento* that resulted in the establishment of a military directory.

Although this movement was wholly monarchical in character it soon became obvious that the King and the General were not complementary. There existed between the two men an antipathy which was to have the most profound and unfortunate consequences, and which was to be one of the main causes of the fall of the monarchy. The relations between a sovereign and a powerful minister necessarily require careful adjustment, but that they may be cordial is proved by such notable combinations as those of Louis XIII and Richelieu, and Victor Emmanuel II and Cavour. On the other hand, the harm that may be done where sympathy does not exist is shown in the cases of the Emperor Wilhelm II and Bismarck, and King Constantine and Venizelos. Primo de Rivera had one serious defect in his character, and that was his failure to appreciate the force of tradition. He thus tended to ignore the Crown, and, on one occasion at least, had toyed with the idea of replacing King Alfonso by the Infante Don Juan. Later, the relations of the two men, though never cordial, improved somewhat, but the result of their misunderstanding was in the long run that the King received all the blame, and none of the credit, for the acts of the directory.

That the administration of General Primo de Rivera conferred great benefits upon Spain is hardly likely to be seriously disputed. In the first place it restored Spanish prestige in Morocco, and the General pacified the Riff so that it became as safe as any province of Spain itself. He enforced law and order throughout the Peninsula, so that during his rule Spain was one of the most peaceful countries in Europe, and all this was done without any interference with the social liberty of the individual. New roads were made, existing communications were improved out of all recognition, and vast irrigation schemes were put into execution. The most friendly relations were established with Latin America, and so high did Spain stand in the counsels of the world that she was elected to a semi-permanent seat on the Council of the League of Nations. Indeed, for a brief space it seemed as if Spain was once again to be a Great Power. Unfortunately, as it is with men so it is with regimes: the evil that they do lives after them, while the good is forgotten, and this has been the fate of the Spanish directory. It made singularly few mistakes, but they were serious ones, and they had fatal consequences.

The initial blunder was the omission to get the *coup d'état* ratified by the Cortes. So overwhelmingly was public opinion on the side of General Primo de Rivera that he would have secured an enormous majority had he demanded full powers, and in that case he would have been able to transform Spain at his will without laying either the King or himself open to the charge of illegality. The failure to adopt such a course was largely due to the General's ignorance of, and contempt for, Parliamentary procedure: it was widely believed in Spain that the Cortes was an effete institution which had had its day, and the General undoubtedly held this view himself. The lack of sympathy with his master was also a secondary cause of his neglect of the Cortes. King Alfonso knew that one day opinion would change, and that as he had taken an oath to respect the constitution, while Primo de Rivera had not, it was he who would be held responsible for the breach of it. The two men were, however, unhappily too far apart to agree, and it would almost certainly have cost the King his throne to have insisted upon the convocation of the Cortes, though, in the end, his neglect to do so had much to do with achieving the same result. King Alfonso considered that the constitution was suspended, and such was the case, but, as it contained no provision for its temporary suspension, he was in law, acting in an unconstitutional manner. Of course, the constitution had so often been disregarded in the past that one more violation of it did not seem to matter, but in this case it eventually placed a very effective weapon in the hands of the enemies of the throne.

A second mistake related to the army. After the establishment of the directory it was universally hoped and believed that the latest *pronunciamiento* would prove to be the last. With the victorious close of the war in Morocco an excellent opportunity presented itself for the abolition of conscription, and for the reform of the army as a voluntary professional force on the then British model. Such a step would at once have provided the monarchy with a shield that would have protected it in every emergency, and it would have earned the undying gratitude of the poorer classes, who have always regarded conscription as an intolerable burden. On the other hand, the maintenance of a large and useless army was not only a very great drain upon the national finances, but was also a direct inducement to ambitious generals to play a part in politics. Even the directory, with a soldier at its head, was continually in difficulties with the army. Had it been reformed along the lines already mentioned, its efficiency would have been increased, and the security of the throne ensured. Why this was not done it is impossible to conjecture, and the reason is probably to be found in the strained relations that existed between the King and his minister.

The end of the directory came at the beginning of 1930, when General Primo de Rivera, whose health was giving way under the strain of his position, realized that he could no longer depend upon the army. In his perplexity, due to his illness, he instituted a referendum of the commanders of the various military districts as to the advisability of his retention of office: this expedient had been adopted in Portugal a few months earlier by General Carmona, and it may well be that General Primo de Rivera was influenced by this example. Such a step was, of course, a violation of the royal prerogative, and the King had no choice but to dismiss the minister. The General, it may be added, was the first to acknowledge the mistake he had made, and he did so in a manner that redounded to his credit. He then left Spain for Paris, where he died a few weeks later.

The departure of Primo de Rivera from the political scene left two courses open to King Alfonso. He could either establish a royal dictatorship, as had recently been done by King Alexander of Yugoslavia, or he could attempt to return to normal constitutional conditions at the earliest possible moment. The decision was the most momentous that the monarch had been forced to take throughout the course of his reign, and it was the more unfortunate that only twelve months earlier death had robbed him of the wisest of his counsellors, that is to say of his mother, Queen Maria Cristina, who had guided her adopted country through so many storms.

The first alternative had much to recommend it. Spain was overwhelmingly monarchical, and those who were ready to conspire against the King's ministers might well hesitate to attack the King himself. It would admittedly have been to stake everything on a single throw, but this risk had to be taken whatever line was adopted. On the other hand, the whole tradition of the reigning branch of the House of Bourbon was against autocracy, and those who in another country would have supported their monarch in such a policy, in Spain were the adherents of the Carlist claimant, Don Jaime. King Alfonso, therefore, determined to retrace his steps, and General Berenguer was appointed to succeed General Primo de Rivera, while a speedy return to the old constitution now became the order of the day. Whatever may be urged against this policy on the score of political strategy, it is surely a complete answer to those who accuse King Alfonso of a determination to destroy the constitution at all costs. A monarch who had such an end in view would hardly have appointed a Prime Minister with instructions to set the old constitutional machinery in motion again at the earliest possible moment.

The new administration had not been in office for more than a few weeks before the chaotic political condition of the country became painfully apparent. The Government of the directory had broken the old Conservative and Liberal parties, and only the purely revolutionary organizations remained intact, if underground. General Berenguer, to give him his due, appreciated these facts, and he wished to hold the elections before the Left had gathered sufficient strength to become a real menace to the existing order. In this desire he was opposed by certain monarchist politicians who wished, by first of all removing the officials appointed by the directory, to "jerrymander" the constituencies in such a way as to secure the return of a majority of their own adherents, and in this manner to enable them to become the arbiters of their country's destiny. In vain the new Prime Minister argued that the only way to avert revolution was to elect a Cortes at the earliest possible moment, and thus to restore legality in the most favourable conditions for the Crown. The politicians, on the contrary, only looked upon the throne as a pawn in their own game, and regarded no other interest than that which they fondly believed to be their own. They refused to listen to General Berenguer, and by representing that the only constitutional course was to hold the local elections first, they unfortunately gained the ear of the King. In this way the General Election was repeatedly postponed throughout the year 1930, while the Left gained in strength every day by asserting that the Government never intended to hold the elections at all.

At this point there took place an insurrection at Jaca, and the consequent proclamation of a state of siege, with the result that a further postponement of the appeal to the country became necessary. By this time the politicians had decided to get rid of General Berenguer altogether, as an obstacle in their path, and so they bluntly declared that they would not take part in the elections even when they were held. This action certainly succeeded in its object of bringing about the fall of General Berenguer, but it sealed the fate of the monarchy itself, which may be said to have collapsed because of the selfishness of those very politicians who most loudly proclaimed themselves its supporters. Nevertheless it is impossible to acquit the

Prime Minister himself of a considerable amount of blame. The probity of General Berenguer was above question, but he was never the man to exercise effective control over others, and he was as little able to check such old hands as the Conde de Romanones in the field of politics as he had been capable of making General Silvestre obey his orders in the mountains of the Riff ten years before. Unfortunately, too, neither he nor his Royal master realized that these selfsame politicians no longer had any followers worth the name, and not the least serious of the many mistakes made at this time was that of taking the old party hacks at their own valuation.

The resignation of General Berenguer was followed by the return to power, under the Premiership of Admiral Aznar, of the old politicians whom the vast majority of Spaniards, whatever their political opinions, hoped the directory had driven out of public life for ever. Back they all came at the King's request, and from the moment that they were seen trooping once more into the Royal Palace at Madrid the advent of the republic was a mere matter of time. The traditional defenders of the throne had little stomach for a fight to protect those whom they profoundly mistrusted, while the revolutionaries gleefully pointed out that the Crown had now so closely associated itself with the "old gang" that it was hopeless to attempt to get rid of the one without also abolishing the other. They had, in fact, managed, partly by their own skill but chiefly owing to the blunders of General Berenguer, to unite against the monarchy all those who had disapproved of the directory, all who had lost their jobs under the administration of its successor, and all who were determined to prevent the government falling once more into the hands of the old politicians. It was a masterpiece of political strategy, though this cannot disguise the fact that had King Alfonso possessed reasonably competent advisers it would have failed.

Nevertheless there was as yet no outward sign of the storm which was so soon to break. The Queen returned from a visit to England, and both at the station in Madrid and during the progress through the streets she and the King were greeted with the most tumultuous reception. A week before the elections was Easter Sunday, and the elaborate ceremonial associated with that event at the Spanish Court was carried out without a hitch, in the midst of popular approval. The Spaniard was apparently quite ready to acclaim the King one day and to vote republican the next, so that in the circumstances it is hardly surprising that no Power abroad, with the exception of the Holy See, should have foreseen what was about to happen.

Such was the position when the local lections were held on April 12th, 1931. Of the councillors elected no less than 22,150 were monarchists, as against 5,875 republicans. With the exception of the four Catalan provinces, Huesca, and Biscay, the result was wholly favourable to the existing order, though it is true that its opponents had won a majority in most of the larger towns. In effect, the voting was a warning that the country did not want the old politicians back in office. but it was nothing more. In these circumstances what it might have been expected that the ministry would do was to proclaim martial law in those towns where there was any possibility of trouble, and then, when order had been restored, to have placed its resignation in the hands of the King. What it did was something very different, namely to lose its head. The Prime Minister declared to the press that the country had gone republican overnight: General Berenguer, who was Minister for War, without consulting his colleagues in the Cabinet, issued a memorandum to the Captains-General throughout Spain of which the Madrid correspondent of *The Times* wrote that "if the republican committee itself had been called upon to circularize the military commanders, it could hardly have drawn up instructions better calculated to serve the purpose of paving the way for a peaceful monarchist surrender"; and, finally, General Sanjurjo, who commanded the Guardia Civil, announced that he was unable to answer for the police.

The monarchy thus collapsed, as in 1868; it was not overthrown. When the result of the elections became known the republicans in Madrid began to demonstrate, and as the authorities did nothing to stop them they became bolder every hour. The King realized that at this stage the monarchy could only be saved by bloodshed, and he refused to order the troops to fire upon his subjects. The republican leaders, for their part, were only anxious to take advantage of the existing situation to get the Royal Family out of Spain before there was a revulsion of feeling in its favour. In consequence, King Alfonso departed by way of Cartagena, and the Queen and her children by that of Irun. It is to be noted that the victorious republicans were in such a hurry to see the monarch on foreign soil that he was able to leave Spain without signing any deed of abdication.

The causes of the fall of the Spanish monarchy have been implicit in the story of its later years, and by no means the least important of them was the fact that King Alfonso had become out of touch with large sections of his subjects, particularly with those who moulded public opinion. He had, over a period of years, made himself so popular in Great Britain and France that it was not realized abroad how isolated he had of late become in his own country.

Then, again, it must be admitted that by his opposition to regionalism he forced the growing demand for decentralization to take an anti-monarchical form. In this matter the King allowed the influence of his Capet and Bourbon ancestors to carry the day against his Habsburg forebears, with the disastrous consequence that the richest part of Spain, namely Catalonia, became the most disaffected. This passion for excessive centralization has wrought havoc in Spain ever since Philip V first crossed the Pyrenees. Is was largely responsible for the loss of America, and it was one of the most potent factors in bringing about the revolution of 1931. Among King Alfonso's many titles was that of Count of Barcelona, and it would not have been difficult to have satisfied Catalan aspirations without in any way weakening the throne. The ministers of the monarchy, including General Primo de Rivera, would have none of it, with the result that Catalonia became another Ireland, and for much the same reason. It was an evil day for the monarchy when Catalan nationalism was allowed to become a weapon in the republican armoury.

The question has often been asked whether King Alfonso would not have done better to have remained in Spain and fought for his throne. The vast majority of his subjects had no desire to abolish the monarchy, and there seems to be no doubt that a large section of the army would have rallied to him. All this is true, but to censure him for not making a stand is to ignore the circumstances in which he was placed. It was clearly quite useless to expect any support from the ministers, who were either paralysed with fright or already making terms with the victorious republicans. The growing isolation of recent years had cut the King off from contact with those who might have saved the situation, and at the supreme moment of his fate the monarch found himself alone. The only counsellor still at the Royal elbow was the Conde de Romanones, and his advice was immediate flight. There is also the character of the King himself to be taken into account in any estimate of what should have been done on this occasion. The proverbial "whiff of grapeshot", or rather its modern equivalent, might well have settled the business, but Don Alfonso was not the man to sit on a throne of which the steps were awash with blood. He had always resolutely set his face against the shooting of Spaniards, and although he may have been wrong in this particular instance, his motives must command respect.

Five years after the fall of the monarchy came the civil war, and this had hardly ended before the Second World War began; in these circumstances the question of a restoration was never a serious issue, and in the meantime, in 1941, King Alfonso died, to be succeeded in his rights by his son, Don Juan. That the majority, perhaps even the large majority, of General Franco's supporters are monarchists is probably true, but although he has proclaimed Spain a monarchy he has taken no steps to fill the vacant throne. For this there are several reasons.

In the first place there is the century-old division in the monarchist ranks, of which it may be well to give some account as it is by no means completely healed. The schism began in the last years of the reign of Ferdinand VII, for that monarch, although he had been married three times, was childless, and his heir was his brother, Don Carlos. In 1830, however, the King entered into matrimony once more, on this occasion with Maria Cristina of Naples, and in due course it was announced that the Queen was pregnant. This event at once raised a constitutional problem of the first importance, and to appreciate the political and personal passions which have since divided

Spanish monarchists it must first of all be remembered that the principle of the succession to the throne had not been settled; indeed it was very much open to question. The *Siete Partidas* of Alfonso X (1252–1284) had recognized the right of females to succeed to the throne of Castille and Leon in default of male heirs of an equally near degree of consanguinity, and that this right had also been admitted in practice is proved by the succession of Isabella I: it was recognized, too, in Aragon for the claim of Charles I (better known as the Emperor Charles V) was through his mother, Juana the Mad. With the advent of the Bourbons at the beginning of the eighteenth century a change was made, and in 1713 Philip V introduced the so-called Salic Law, which established the French procedure.

The position was still further complicated by the fact that for some obscure reason Charles IV in 1789 convoked the Cortes in secret session, and on his initiative a resolution was passed asking him to revert to the old order of succession, but the necessary decree was never promulgated. In March, 1830, Ferdinand VII promulgated the Pragmatic Sanction of Charles IV, and in June of the same year he made a will in which he left the crown to his unborn child. Don Carlos could not, and did not, object to the principle of leaving the crown by will, for it was owing to an act of this nature on the part of Charles II that the Bourbons were in the Peninsula at all, but he protested against the promulgation of the Pragmatic Sanction. He denied that it was geniune, and declared that, in any case, since he was alive at the date of its enactment it could not be retrospective. Ferdinand at one time gave way, and revoked the Pragmatic Sanction, but he eventually destroyed the revocation, and when a daughter, Isabella, was born, he recognized her as his heir. In 1833 the King died, and thus, in his own words, the cork was removed from the fermenting and surcharged bottle of Spain. As Isabella II his daughter succeeded to the throne.

In retrospect, it is impossible not to regret that Don Carlos did not succeed his brother, Ferdinand VII. Had this happened the monarchists would not have been divided, and Spain would probably have been spared three civil wars as well as two most unfortunate republican experiences. Furthermore, she lost in the Carlist claimants the services of monarchs of considerable ability and of high character, while she would have avoided two long and disastrous minorities. The interference of the army in public life dates from the death of Ferdinand, and the *pronunciamiento* would in all probability not have been so prominent a feature of modern history had the throne been occupied by Don Carlos and his heirs. What the July Revolution of 1830 was to the monarchy of France the disinheriting of Don Carlos was to that of Spain.

These events were no mere memory to the Spanish monarchists in 1931. As had been the case with the First Republic, so the advent of the Second witnessed a revival of Carlism, though with a marked difference which undoubtedly strengthened its appeal. Few Carlists in 1931 really hoped to restore the legitimate heir to the throne, for he was eighty-one years of age and he was the last of his line. What they were determined to effect was the incorporation in some future Spanish constitution of the religious and political principles which were the basis of their creed, and for the abandonment of which they could not forgive the monarchists who supported King Alfonso XIII. The Carlists, or Traditionalists as they came to be called, provided General Franco with some of his best troops in the *requetes*, and their influence in his counsels has always been considerable. To-day both King Alfonso and the last Carlist claimant, Don Alfonso Carlos, are both dead, and on every ground of descent the rightful King of Spain is Don Juan, but there are still Traditionalists who are unwilling to accept him, and their attitude provides General Franco with both a reason and an excuse for his delay in filling the vacant Spanish throne.

Probably, however, at the root of this delay are the unsatisfactory personal relations between Don Juan and General Franco, which recall those existing between King Alfonso XIII and General Primo de Rivera. There would appear to be so complete a lack of sympathy between the two men as to preclude any co-operation between them in the event of a restoration of the monarchy. Don Juan fears that he would be expected to play Victor Emmanuel III to Franco's Mussolini, while the General is apprehensive that once in the saddle Don Juan would dismiss him as his father dismissed Primo de Rivera. Had the two men any liking for, or trust in, one another, this difficulty could easily be surmounted, but in existing circumstance the personal factor is a big obstacle in the way of the restoration of Don Juan.

Lastly there is to be taken into account the hesitation of the vast majority of Spaniards to make any change in case it may prove to be for the worse. They remember the disorders which marked the last years of King Alfonso's reign, and which led through the chaos of the Second Republic to the horrors of the civil war. They would like to see a King back again in Madrid, but with Communism menacing the world they feel it safer to wait until the forces in Spain making for stability are more firmly established.

Meanwhile Spain remains a monarchy without a King.

II

THE ITALIAN MONARCHY

Italy a New State with an Old Civilization—Weakness of the Monarchical Principle—
Position of the Papacy—The House of Savoy—Reign of King Humbert I—King Victor
Emmanuel III and the First World War—The Fascist March on Rome—The Monarchy
under Fascism—Mussolini—The King's Blunders—Weakness of the Monarchy—King
Humbert II—Results of the Plebiscite—Some Reflections on the Distribution of Votes—
Establishment of a Republic

AT THE very beginning of the twentieth century, on July 29th, 1900, King Humbert I of Italy was murdered at Monza, near Milan, while he was standing acknowledging the cheers of the crowd at the close of a ceremony which he had just attended, and the long reign of his only son, King Victor Emmanuel III, began. The House of Savoy had slowly through the centuries raised itself from insignificance to the kingship of United Italy, but in less than fifty years from the tragedy at Monza it was to take the road of exile. It is easy to ascribe this change of fortune to the mistakes of the man who had that day succeeded to the throne, and though he must bear his share of the blame more than one of the forces which brought the monarchy down had its roots in a somewhat remoter past.

It must never be forgotten that Italy is a new state with an old civilization, and in this combination lies the answer to much that is otherwise inexplicable, not least where the monarchy is concerned. A hundred years ago she was a mere geographical expression, and although the Grand Duchy of Tuscany or the Kingdom of the Two Sicilies may seem as remote to the modern Englishman as Mercia or Wessex, they are quite close in point of time: there must, for example, be not a few Italians still alive to-day who have heard the Austrian trumpets echo across the lagoon at Venice. In England and Spain, as we have seen, the national tradition was monarchical, but in this divided Italy there was no national tradition, and local traditions were very often quite definitely republican in their origin.

This weakness of the monarchical principle was due to the fact that outside Piedmont it was represented by the foreigner and by the Pope, both of whom were looked upon as the main obstacles to the attainment of unity. In these circumstances it is hardly surprising that monarchy came to be regarded as synonymous with the existing order, and republicanism with its abolition. During the generation that followed the fall of Napoleon the High Priest of Legsitimism was Metternich, and he was the minister of the alien ruler whose troops held Milan and Venice in thrall. The King of Naples and the Duke of Parma were Spaniards, while the Grand Duke of Tuscany and the Duke of Modena were Austrians, so that it is hardly surprising that opposition to the rule of the foreigner should have assumed a republican form, quite apart from the fact that the protagonist of Italian nationalism at that time was so convinced an enemy of monarchy as Giuseppe Mazzini. Earlier still, there can be no doubt that the terrific struggle between Empire and Papacy had weakened the monarchical principle, while the stability that for so long characterized the republics of Venice and Genoa was in marked contrast with the turmoil that was often the lot of the other Italian states.

In actual fact, of course, these states were not legitimate monarchies, so much as tyrannies, in the Greek sense of the term, where the succession was precarious in the extreme, and the only real exception was Piedmont. Such families as the Visconti were monarchical solely in the etymological meaning of the word, and there is no evidence that they ever gained the affection of those over whom they ruled. The same applies to the Medici, whom the Florentines expelled on more than one occasion, and whom they finally tolerated because there did not appear to be any alternative that was not definitely worse. The Estensi, it must be admitted, do not come into the same category, and more nearly approximate to the House of Savoy; indeed, for one fleeting moment there was a chance that Italy might be united under their sceptre, and so long as the family was still represented in the male line the House of Este never lost its hold upon popular imagination. Elsewhere there was no incarnation of the principle of true monarchy that could appeal to the loyalty of the patriotic Italian.

As for the Papacy, it was a theocracy rather than a monarchy. The Pope was also recognized as King in his own dominions, but it was as the successor of St. Peter that he was generally regarded by his subjects. It was in the nature of things quite impossible to dissociate him from the Church of which he was the head, and it was as Catholics, not as *papalini*, that those who lived in the States of the Church accepted his rule. The whole question of the Temporal Power was bound up, not with the advantages or disadvantages of the monarchical principle, but with the position of the Church in the world, and no one ever took the Pope seriously as a temporal monarch in the ordinary sense, at any rate in his own dominions. Furthermore, until 1523 he was often a foreigner, and even after that date he was frequently a native of some distant part of the Peninsula which seemed as remote as the Indies to the majority of the inhabitants of the States of the Church. Such being the case, it is in no way surprising that when the struggle for independence began it should have been republican in its nature in all that wide area which was ruled by the Pope, and in Romagna, where Mussolini was born, in particular this sentiment died hard. Whether or not Italy was naturally republican she had, outside Piedmont, little or no experience of the working of monarchical institutions in a manner that was not essentially repugnant to the national sentiment and aspirations.

In the thirties and forties of the nineteenth century there were three main schools of thought among those who were working for Italian independence, and their doctrines have not entirely lost their influence a hundred years later. First of all there were the federalists, inspired by Vincenzo Gioberti, who desired to see Italy united in a federation of which the Pope should be President. This scheme, of course, would have left the individual states as they were, and for this reason it made no inconsiderable appeal to monarchists throughout the peninsula. Its weakness lay in the fact that it presupposed a Pope who was willing to offend Austria, the leading Catholic Power, for the sake of the freedom of Italy, an impossible decision to expect any man in such a position to take. The election of Pius IX in 1846, as the successor of the pro-Austrian Gregory XVI, temporarily raised the hopes of Gioberti and his followers, for the new Pope was favourable to the cause of Italian unity, and it is even said that he had been a *carbonaro* in his youth. Before long, however, he realized that Gioberti's scheme was impracticable, and when the final decision had to be made Pius ranged himself on the side of

Austria and the existing order. From that moment the federal solution ceased to be practical politics.

In a different form the idea of the Papacy playing a prominent part in Italian politics was put forward by Don Sturzo and the *partito popolare* after the First World War, but it was frowned upon by the Vatican and Don Sturzo's party was suppressed. More recently, since the fall of the House of Savoy, it has been argued that there is no necessity to restore the King since Italy already has a monarchy in the Papacy, a point of view which might be not inaccurately described as neo-Giobertian.

The failure of the federalists left the stage clear for the second group, namely Mazzini and the republicans. Their plan was to overthrow the Temporal Power of the Pope, expel the existing dynasties and the Austrians, and create a unitary republic. They had their chance in 1848, and after considerable bloodshed they, too, failed miserably. It is one of the ironies of history that when Italy became the unitary republic of Mazzini's dreams the majority in the Chamber should have been composed of Christian Democrats devoted to the Holy See.

When, in 1849, the Gianiculo passed from the hands of Garibaldi into those of the French, the real victor was neither Louis Napoleon nor Pius IX, but Victor Emmanuel II and Cavour, who now became the only hope of every Italian patriot. This third group had not been very strong until then, but the logic of events made all who were not fanatics rally round Piedmont, and those who realized the impossibility of any other solution now began to work for this end. At their head was Cavour, one of the greatest statesmen of all time. In due course he succeeded in his object, and, in 1870, Victor Emmanuel II, as King of Italy, took possession of Rome as his capital.

In connection with the unification of Italy under the House of Savoy two aspects of this event must not be ignored. The first is that Italy was not created by the monarchy as had been the case with England, France, and Spain; the monarchical form of government was adopted because no other was immediately suitable, and because since it had been proved that while a republic would divide it was hoped that a monarchy might unite. In short, recourse had been had to the monarchy on grounds of expediency, not of principle. Secondly, hereditary monarch though he was, Victor Emmanuel II had only ascended from the throne of Sardinia to that of Italy by overturning a number of lesser thrones which lay in his path. Thus, from the beginning there was little of the proverbial divinity to hedge the monarchs of the new Italian kingdom.

When Victor Emmanuel II died in 1878 Italy was a Great Power in name, but she was a long way from being such in fact, and his son and successor, Humbert I, spent twenty-two very difficult years upon the throne. As has been shown, political conditions in the new kingdom were unnatural, for the Right, to which the monarchy should have been able to look for support, was "Black" as a general rule, that is to say it was grouped round the Pope, and refused to have any dealings with the Savoyard. Then, again, the intoxication of the *Risorgimento* was over, and only the headache remained. To the generation which had grown up in the struggle for independence life seemed very drab, and not a few foreign observers declared, with considerable truth, that Italy had been made too easily and too quickly. Abroad, too, one humiliation succeeded another, and it was the misfortune of Humbert to see his country's prestige reach its nadir. The French occupation of Tunis in 1881 was a reverse which drove Italy into the arms of Germany and

Austria, and to this was added fifteen years later the shame of the defeat of the Italian troops by the Abyssinians at Adowa. On all sides there was a feeling of disillusionment, and, as so often in the period immediately following a revolution, in politics the scum rose to the surface. The only statesman of Humbert's reign who was of the first class was Crispi, and when a more or less inadvertent act of bigamy was proved against him, he was forced to retire from public life after the catastrophe of Adowa.

Nor was this the sum of the difficulties which Humbert had to face, for the growing industrialization of parts of Italy had given birth to Socialism of a most violent type. Nowhere was there stability, and in this soil terrorism took root. The Italian anarchist became a familiar and dreaded figure both in the Old World and the New, until in due course Humbert himself became the victim of his bullets.

Troubled as was the reign of Humbert I, it was peaceful compared with that of King Victor Emmanuel III, who was in any case by no means as forceful a personality as his father. The disruptive tendencies became ever more marked, and foreign observers began to question how much longer Italy would hold together. The industrial situation grew steadily worse, and revolutionary strikes, which paralyzed the whole economic life of the country, became the order of the day. During this period the real ruler of the country was neither the King, nor Parliament, nor the electorate, but Giovanni Giolitti, who was dictator in all but name. He made and unmade ministries, jerrymandered the constituencies, and administered Italy in a manner upon which Boss Croker himself could not have improved. Unfortunately for himself, he never realized that economic ills cannot be cured by political remedies, and so the

Socialist menace grew apace. While the party game was being played in the Chamber according to the rules laid down by Giolitti, revolution was stalking the streets of the great cities, and such was the situation when, in August, 1914, the world found itself at war.

It will hardly be denied that at this critical time the King however alarmed he might be at the progress of events, continued to observe the constitution both in the letter and in the spirit. Giolitti was hostile to participation in the war, so no great opposition was displayed to the official refusal of Italy to take the field by the side of Germany and Austria. It was, however, different when the demand for intervention against the Central Powers, largely voiced by Benito Mussolini, began to be made, for the whole influence of Giolitti was thrown into the scale in favour of neutrality. By the spring of 1915 the vast majority of Italians were in favour of war, and the Prime Minister, Antonio Salandra, had already concluded the Treaty of London with the Allied Powers. This was the moment chosen by Giolitti, who was acting in close collaboration with the German ambassador, to precipitate a Cabinet crisis as a last desperate effort to avoid intervention. The Prime Minister resigned, and it seemed as if Giolitti had triumphed, and Italy would remain neutral.

For the first time since he had come to the throne King Victor Emmanuel took the initiative, and his action has not since been seriously called in question. He interpreted the wishes of the country far better than the Chamber had done, and he refused to accept the resignation of Salandra, who accordingly remained in office, and war was duly declared against Austria. Throughout the period of hostilities the King remained with the army, and he did not return to Rome until the victory had been won. Indeed, during these years the popularity of the House of Savoy reached its apogee during the present century, for not only was the King continually visiting the front line but his cousin, the Duke of Aosta, commanded an army, while another member of the Royal Family, and Duke of the Abruzzi, was for a time commander-in-chief of the navy. All this, it may be observed, was in marked contrast with the reluctance of the deputies to don a uniform at all.

Four years after the end of the First World War came the Fascist march on Rome when the King was again forced to take independent action which has ever since given rise to a great deal of acrimonious controversy, First of all, however, it will be as well to recall the actual events of that momentous autumn. On September 29th, at a Fascist conference at Udine, Mussolini for the first time openly declared himself a monarchist. It is true that for some years his republicanism had been traditional rather than active, but this declaration swung many waverers over to the Fascist cause. On the night of October 27th the march on Rome began. The first blow was struck by Farinacci, who seized Cremona, and by noon of the 28th the strategic centre of Italy was in Fascist hands, as well as the great towns of Milan, Florence, and Naples. The way was now clear for the second stage of the revolution, namely the occupation of the capital itself. The railway system was wholly under Fascist control, and it was used to concentrate some hundred thousand men at the gates of Rome, where they were massed at Santa Marinella, Monterotondo, and Tivoli for the final attack. Another hundred thousand were gathering in reserve at Foligno, and civil war seemed imminent.

Luigi Facta, the Prime Minister, was taken by surprise by the Fascist *coup*, and he seems to have lost his head. He ordered the immediate arrest of Mussolini and his principal supporters, and he issued a decree establishing martial law throughout the country. Hardly had this last action been taken than Facta was reminded that it was illegal without the royal assent, and when he went to the King to obtain this he was met with a blank refusal. The decree was thereupon withdrawn, and Facta resigned. King Victor Emmanuel has been much criticized for the attitude he adopted, but history cannot be read backwards. No one in 1922 could foresee the German alliance and the humiliation which it would entail. Far outside the Fascist ranks there was widespread support for Mussolini, and had the King supported Facta it was at least doubtful whether the army would have stood by him. The most probable outcome would have been a civil war ending in a Fascist victory.

What is not always appreciated is that the King was careful to observe the usual constitutional forms on the occasion of a ministerial crisis. He commissioned Salandra to form a Cabinet with Fascist support, whereupon Salandra promptly placed two or three portfolios at Mussolini's disposal, an offer which was as promptly refused. By the morning of October 29th it was clear that there was only one solution, and on that day the Fascist leader received instructions from the King to form a ministry. He accordingly came from Milan to Rome, and proceeded to the Quirinal, whence he duly appeared as Prime Minister of Italy. It is to be noted that, by way of contrast with General Primo de Rivera, one of his first acts was to secure a vote of confidence from the Chamber.

We are still too near the Fascist regime to obtain either an objective or an impartial view of its relations with the monarchy. These would, however, appear to have been much closer and more cordial in its earlier, than in its later, days. Soon after this arrival in office

Mussolini himself defined the throne as *"simbolo della Patria, simbolo della perpetuità della Patria"*, and in his first speech to the Chamber after the march on Rome he said: "I believe I am interpreting the thoughts of the majority of the Chamber, or at all events of the majority of the nation, when I turn in homage to the King, who refused to adopt useless and reactionary measures, who prevented the outbreak of civil war, and who allowed the mighty tide of Fascism to flow into the dry veins of a Parliamentary State". The Fascist rank and file were much slower in reaching this conclusion than their leader, and many of them never reached it at all, so that although they accepted the monarchy from the point of view of expediency, it was, as Major J. S. Barnes justly observed in his *Fascism*, "very much in the spirit in which the prophet Samuel reluctantly condescended to the anointing of Saul as the first King of Israel". There was, in effect, toleration of, but no great enthusiasm for, the throne.

The constitutional position of the Crown, however, was soon modified to suit the new order. Previously the King had selected the Prime Minister in much the same way as the President of the French Republic was accustomed to do, that is to say when an administration fell the monarch entered upon a series of consultations, first of all with the Presidents of the Senate and Chamber, and then with the leaders of the various parties, with a view to finding someone who could collect a sufficient majority to keep him in office for a time. Under Fascism the Head of the Government was made responsible, not to the Chamber, but to the King, who appointed him after selection from a panel presented by the Fascist Grand Council, and it was the Head of the Government who nominated and dismissed the other ministers. The Grand Council had also to be consulted in all constitutional matters, so that any proposals affecting the succession to the throne, the powers of the Crown, or the royal prerogative came before it.

For some years this arrangement would appear to have worked and the King was as much, or as little, in evidence under the Fascist regime as he had been under its Parliamentary predecessor. At any rate there were not even rumours of any serious difference between monarch and dictator, and the cafés of Rome, unlike those of contemporary Madrid, did not resound with stories of dissension in the highest circles. It may be that Mussolini was as yet none too sure of his position, and was unwilling to do anything which might alienate those who only supported him because of his conversion to monarchism; it may even be, unfashionable as it has now become to credit the Duce with any decent feeling at all, that in this springtime of Fascist power he really was actuated by a belief in the mission of the House of Savoy as unifying force in Italian politics.

What must never be forgotten in endeavouring to arrive at the truth in connection with the relations between King Victor Emmanuel and Mussolini is that until Italy entered the Second World War on the side of Germany there was no serious criticism in the country of the monarch's co-operation with the dictator. Very few Italians, save those who went into exile, really objected to Fascism as such, though quite a number were most unwilling to see their country dragged into war against Great Britain, with whom it had such long and intimate connections. For the rest, what made Fascism unpopular, was not its tyranny but its failure, and when it had palpably failed, with the most disastrous consequences to Italy, there was a general desire to find a scapegoat. King Victor Emmanuel is roundly denounced to-day for not having broken with the Duce, but at what date and on what issue is very rarely stated by his critics.

It is, however, by no means improbable that the attitude of Mussolini towards the monarchy underwent a change as a result of his association with Hitler. Friedelind Wagner, in *The Royal Family of Bayreuth*, throws an interesting light upon the Führer's views on such matters. "That same evening Hitler told us about his recent visit to Mussolini and his first contact with the ceremonials of a Royal court. When he wanted to retire on the first night of the visit, the Lord-Chamberlain with an elaborate branched candlestick in one hand, led a slow-motion procession through miles of regal halls including the throne room. The next day Hitler told Mussolini that if this nonsense wasn't stopped he wouldn't stay another night". On the same occasion Hitler observed, "How Mussolini endures it, I don't see. I told him again and again to get rid of all this Royalty, but he says the time hasn't come yet". All the same it is more than probable that the Führer's advice was not forgotten. By this time megalomania had claimed Mussolini, and he may easily have come to resent the fact while Hitler was the first man in Germany he was not in the same position in his country.

With the coming of the Second World War the Italian monarchy receded ever further into the background. There can be little doubt that the King, in common with many of his subjects, viewed with extreme disfavour the entry of Italy into the conflict on the side of Germany, but, again like many of his subjects, the King took no definite action. In fact it was already too late for him to do so. Marshal Badoglio, in his *Italy in the Second World War*, shows how the royal power had shrunk to nothing even before hostilities began. "The King told me during a conversation which I had with him in 1943 in Brindisi that Mussolini had never informed him of his intention to form an alliance with Hitler. It was only when the agreement was concluded and signed that Mussolini decided to notify the King. Now Article 5 of the constitution reads: 'Executive power appertains exclusively to the King . . . he declares war, makes treaties of peace, alliance and commerce. . . .' His Majesty showed his very deep resentment at these proceedings and expressed to Mussolini his anger at such a violation of the constitution. 'It was not possible to undo what had been done', added the King, 'without causing serious difficulties'." All the same, on June 4th, 1940, Mussolini obtained from the King the command of the armed forces in the field.

For the next three years King Victor Emmanuel remained completely in the background, but when disaster after disaster had overtaken the Italian armies in every theatre, he intervened decisively, though the actual background of this intervention is still somewhat obscure. To quote the King's own words as reproduced by Marshal Badoglio: "This morning (*i.e.* July 25th, 1943) Mussolini asked me for an interview which I fixed for this afternoon at 4.0 p.m. at this villa. When he arrived Mussolini told me that a meeting of the Fascist Grand Council had been held and had passed a vote of censure on him, but he believed that this resolution was not in order. I replied at once that I did not agree with him; the Grand Council was an organ of State which he himself had created by means of a law which had been passed by the Chamber and the Senate; therefore every decision of the Grand Council was valid. 'Then according to Your Majesty I ought to resign', he said with considerable violence. 'Yes', I answered, and told him that I forthwith accepted his resignation. When he heard this Mussolini collapsed. 'Then my ruin is complete', he muttered hoarsely".

In view of the prominent part which the King thus played in the last resort in the overthrow of the Fascist regime why was it that the House of Savoy became itself so fatally compromised in that overthrow? The question is not an easy one to answer, but a few possible explanations can be put forward in the absence of that fuller information which the passage of time alone can provide.

In the first place there is the character of the Italian people to be taken into account. Contrary to the view commonly held abroad they are not, once their immediate anger has spent itself, vindictive, but, like the commonalty all over the world, they must have their scapegoat. They had believed in Mussolini and though to a lesser extent, in Fascism: when they were undeceived they wanted someone to blame for not having opened their eyes sooner, and the most convenient whipping-boy was the monarchy, which, for reasons already mentioned, had no very deep roots in many parts of the country.

Then, again, King Victor Emmanuel made a number of serious mistakes, though in slight extenuation of them it must be remembered that he was a man of seventy-four when he dismissed Mussolini. He never seems to have realized the extent to which he was compromised with Fascism in the eyes of the public, or to have imagined that his subjects would so soon be clamouring for a scapegoat. What he should have done was what his great-grandfather, Charles Albert, did on the morrow of Novara, that is to say abdicate in favour of his eldest son. What he did was, contrary to the advice of the most devoted supporters of his dynasty, to hold on to power for a year, and even then the Prince of

Piedmont, Humbert, was only appointed Lieutenant-General of the Kingdom (June 5th, 1944). It was not until June, 1946, that King Victor Emmanuel III finally abdicated, and by then it was far too late to save the throne. For almost the first time in history the head of the House of Savoy had failed in that sureness of touch which had for a thousand years been the outstanding characteristic of the dynasty, and so he brought down in a few months the edifice which his ancestors had so carefully and so painfully erected during the course of centuries. Curiously enough, his relative, King Leopold III of the Belgians, was in different circumstances also giving evidence that he had not inherited the shrewdness of another Royal House famous for its just appraisal of an intricate political situation, namely that of Saxe-Coburg and Gotha.

A further source of weakness, as the plebiscite was conclusively to prove, was the establishment by Mussolini of a Fascist republic behind the German Lines in the North of Italy; it is true that this regime did not last long but it lasted long enough for some of the mud which was thrown at the House of Savoy to stick. Particularly was this the case in Piedmont, the old home of the dynasty, where the denigration of the Royal Family had a very considerable effect on a population which would otherwise have been among its strongest supporters.

What is not quite clear is why there should have been a plebiscite at all, and it is difficult to resist the conclusion that it might have been avoided had King Victor Emmanuel III abdicated immediately after the dismissal of Mussolini. As it was King Humbert II never had a chance, for he was only on the throne a month before he was voted off it. In his earlier years he had been none too popular, but his known dislike of Mussolini had caused a change of feeling in his favour as the Fascist regime began to decline in public estimation. Indeed, it is by no means improbable that if the plebiscite had been postponed for another six months or so the result might have been different. All the same it must be admitted that the plebiscite was conducted fairly; a great deal more fairly, it may be added, that those which had seated the House of Savoy on the throne of United Italy in an earlier generation.

It took place on June 2nd, 1946, when there were 12,717,923 votes cast for the establishment of a republic against 10,719,284 for the retention of the monarchy. The geographical distribution of these votes is by no means uninteresting: Rome, Naples, Bari, Palermo, and Sardinia were for the King, while Milan, Turin, Genoa, Florence, and Venice preferred a republic. It would appear, too, that the division was by no means a Left versus Right alignment, and a great many of those who voted Christian Democrat at the General Election of April, 1948, must have opted for a republic two years earlier, particularly in Central Italy and Venetia. The old Kingdom of the Two Sicilies is still monarchist to the core, though indifferent as to the particular dynasty that occupies the throne, but there were clearly a large number of voters elsewhere whose "Black" background would not allow them to support the descendant of the man who had despoiled the Pope of his possessions. They were quite prepared to accept the House of Savoy as part of the established order, but to give it active support at the polls was another matter.

So King Humbert II passed into exile, but with the knowledge that on the question of regime Italy is almost equally divided. If and when the republic runs into serious difficulties, either at home or abroad, those 10,719,284 voters will make their influence felt, Meanwhile, they lack a leader.

III

THE GREEK MONARCHY

A Republican Background—Origin of the Greek Monarchy—King George I—His Virtues and Death—Venizelos—The Tragedy of King Constantine—Difficulties and Deposition of King George II—The Greek Republic—Apogee and Decline of Venizelos—Monarchist Revival—Hesitations of Tsaldaris—The Plebiscite—Restoration of King George II— His Difficulties—Metaxas in Power—The Second World War—German Conquest of Greece—Communist Activities—A Disordered Country—The Second Restoration of King George II—His Death—Accession of King Paul

IN THE matter of regime modern Greece presents a paradox for no country possesses so republican a historical background, and yet during the past generation no country has shown itself more devotedly monarchical in spite of every temptation to embrace the extremes both of Right and Left. This fidelity to the Crown is all the more remarkable in view of the fact that Greece has never had a native monarch since her liberation from the Turks at the beginning of the nineteenth century, and the present Royal Family has no Greek blood in its veins. The explanation lies in the procession of able men who have occupied the throne. First of all, however, it is necessary to look back a little.

In the past the Greeks suffered because too much was expected of them by the outside world, for if the result was to cause disappointment abroad there were also unhappy repercussions at home. Colonel Napier wrote of the Philhellenes of the War of Independence that they "came expecting to find the Peloponnesus filled with Plutarch's men", and they were not alone in their mistake. The great days of Greece were remembered, while the demoralizing effect of centuries of Ottoman rule was forgotten, and disillusionment was too often the result. This alternation of hope and despair in the attitude of their foreign friends had unfortunate reactions upon the Greeks themselves. Nor was the attitude of the so-called Protecting Powers, that is to say Great Britain, France, and Russia, calculated to stimulate the centripetal forces in Greece. First of all, in 1832, the country was endowed with a Bavarian prince, Otto, of the tender age of seventeen, as its monarch; but when in due course he began to show himself too patriotic a Greek to suit the convenience of the three Powers he was manoeuvred off the throne. The Greeks were then denied the successor they wanted, and given, in 1863, another youth as their King in the person of Prince George of Denmark. Fortunately he and his dynasty speedily became completely identified with the national interests, but the young kingdom had been given a bad start by its patronizing foreign friends.

King George I of the Hellenes has never yet received the tribute that is his due. He steered his country successfully through crises, internal and external, which she would never otherwise have been able to surmount, and the hold he possessed over his subjects is proved by the fact that he retained his throne in spite of the defeat of his armies by the Turks in 1897 and of the activities of the Military League twelve years later. He died in 1913 by the hand of an assassin in the hour of Greece's triumph, and in his political testament he gave to his son some advice which his successors on the throne have most faithfully followed:

> Love thy beloved little country with thy whole heart;
> be bold, but also patient: never be overhasty; rather let

the night pass before taking thy decision; be not angry, and let not the sun go down upon thy wrath; be calm in thought and mind, and never forget that thou art King of a southern people, whose wrath and excitability are kindled in a moment, and which at such a moment is capable of saying and doing many things which a moment later it will perhaps forget; and remember that it is often better for the King himself to suffer, even morally, rather than the people, whose interests should take precedence of all others.

Not the least of King George's difficulties was the absence during the greater part of his reign of any Greek statesman of the first rank with the exception of Tricoupis. This remarkable man first conceived the idea of an alliance of the Balkan states to drive the Turk out of Europe without the assistance of the Great Powers, but the plan came to nothing in his lifetime because it was betrayed by the Bulgarian Government to the Porte at the moment when it was about to be put into operation.

Towards the end of the reign Venizelos emerged from his native Crete on to the larger stage of Greek politics. For many years he was to be the stormy petrel of the Near East, and he aroused more devotion and more hatred than almost any man of modern times, until, after the failure of his last revolt in the spring of 1935, he took refuge on Italian soil. This is not the place to canvass his virtues and vices, but it may be said without fear of contradiction that he possessed two strongly-marked characteristics—he was very difficult to work with, and for him the means justified the end. He was a political gambler, and he gloried in the fact. All the same he and the new King, Constantine, co-operated to the great advantage of their country on the morrow of the overthrow of the Turks; and in the Second Balkan War, after Bulgaria's treacherous attack upon her allies, the Greek army covered itself with distinction in some particularly severe fighting.

How long monarch and minister would have continued to work together in normal circumstances is a moot point, but unfortunately for them and for Greece the First World War soon involved them in the struggles of others. What followed has been the subject of considerable misrepresentation both in France and in Great Britain.

It is still commonly believed that King Constantine devoted all his energies to sabotaging the efforts of the Allies in the interests of his brother-in-law, the German Emperor, while the Cretan had no other thought than to mobilize the resources of Greece in opposition to the Central Powers. Actually, the situation admits of no such simplification. The King offered to the Allies the plan for an attack upon the Gallipoli Peninsula which had been drawn up by Colonel Metaxas, but neither he nor the Greek General Staff was ever consulted as to the expedition, although they were expected to co-operate in it. It is therefore hardly surprising that when things began to go wrong King Constantine should have told the British military attaché, "I have never heard, and I never read, of a more amateurish method of approaching a serious military enterprise than your people employed at the Dardanelles".

Such candour did little to recommend the Greek monarch to the embarrassed Allies, and they retaliated by making him the scapegoat of their blunders. In this they secured the support of Venizelos, and Greece was soon torn by internal strife. What then occurred is too well known to require detailed description. King Constantine was forcibly deposed by the Allies, among whom France took the lead, and his second son, Alexander, was put on the throne in his place. The overthrow of the Central Powers promised many benefits to Greece, but on the death of King Alexander in 1920 his father was restored, and a divided country saw its armies go down to disaster in Asia Minor. Another revolution brought King George II to the throne, King Constantine having abdicated in his favour, but all real power was in the hands of a revolutionary committee.

During the brief period in 1922-23 during which King George II occupied the throne, his behaviour was, even on the admission of his enemies, that of a patriot and a gentleman. He had accompanied his father into exile in 1917, and when called to succeed him endeavoured to make the best of what was really an impossible situation. There were few insults to which he was not subjected, and when King Constantine died at Palermo the Government of the day refused to allow his son even to fly his flag at half-mast on the palace. When the oligarchy that ruled Greece proceeded to drag the country's name in the mud by executing the former Commander-in-chief in Asia Minor, together with five ex-minsters, the King determined to leave the country, and was only dissuaded from doing so by the representatives of Great Britain and France. Meanwhile, the Greek people were becoming tired of the revolutionary committee, headed by Plastiras and Gonatas, which was governing them, and in October, 1923, Metaxas put himself at the head of a movement for a return to constitutional government. It proved, however, to be premature, and was crushed. There was no evidence that the King had any responsibility, but Gonatas and Plastiras were determined to take advantage of the opportunity to get rid of the monarchy. Accordingly, although the newly-formed republican party failed to secure anything approaching a majority at the ensuing elections the Government requested the King to absent himself from the country during the meeting of the National Assembly which was to decide the future of the dynasty. On December 23rd, 1923, the monarch complied with this request to avoid bloodshed, and departed for Rumania, though without abdicating any of his rights.

After a considerable amount of manoeuvring for position between Venizelos, Cafandaris, and Papanastassiou, and the military and naval chiefs, the Assembly on March 25th, 1924, proclaimed the abolition of the monarchy and the establishment of a parliamentary republic. The following month witnessed a plebiscite, when 758,742 votes were cast for a republic and 325,322 for the monarchy. In spite of the size of the minority it was generally assumed that the question of the regime in Greece had been finally settled. Writers on Greece adopted this tone for many years. Mr. John Mavrogordato, in his *Modern Greece* published in 1931, quoted with approval a statement of Venizelos to the effect that there was "nothing in the situation to warrant either an early or a late restoration of the ex-King George". Two years later, Dr. Otto Ernst, in *Kings in exile*, wrote of King George, "His dynasty hardly comes into consideration for the vacant throne of Greece". Such opinions, far from being exceptional, were the rule.

The Greek republic had a stormy career, and for a brief period, too, there was a dictatorship under General Pangalos, but he was generally considered to have exceeded the limits even of dictatorial power when he attempted to prescribe the length of women's skirts, and compelled the police to equip themselves with tape-measures in order to see that his commands were obeyed: nevertheless he did confer one benefit on Greece, namely the construction of the excellent road which connects Athens with Eleusis. Throughout the republican period the dominant figure was that of Venizelos, whether in or out of office. No impartial person can deny that the Cretan statesman did much for Greece, and all over the country one comes across evidence of his foresight. On the other hand, he was an inveterate intriguer, and long before his death he had become a liability to his fellow-countrymen. As he grew older he was surrounded by an entourage who always represented a situation to him as he wanted it to be. One of the curses of modern Greece has been that so many of her leaders have passed their early days in opposition to an Oriental despotism, and the political habits and outlook thus acquired have remained unaltered for the rest of their lives. So it was with Venizelos, and in old age he reverted to the mentality of his youth. Napoleon remained at heart a Corsican, and the murder of the Duc d'Enghien was an act in the family vendetta between Bonaparte and Bourbon. The last public act of the Cretan, the mad insurrection of March, 1935, was performed in the same spirit as the first, that is to say the seizure of Akroteri thirty-eight years before.

The elections of April, 1928, marked the apogee of Venizelos, for the monarchists only obtained twenty-six seats. From that moment his star began to wane, and his task was rendered still more difficult by the world economic crisis which soon made its appearance. In the spring of 1933 he was so out of favour with the electors that they returned an anti-Venizelist majority of Populists under Tsaldaris, that is to say of old Royalists who had accepted the republic. Venizelos endeavoured to nullify this by a *coup d'état* on the part of Plastiras, but it failed, though it so frightened Tsaldaris that he refused to take any step in the direction of a restoration of the monarchy. In the meantime evidence was accumulating of the growth of Royalist feeling among those who were weary of the eternal party strife, and every time there was an opportunity the Greeks seized it to express their contempt for Venizelos and all his works. In despair of ever returning to office by the votes of his fellow-countrymen, the Liberal leader once more resorted to force and precipitated civil war. This time he was decisively beaten, chiefly by the energy of Generals Condylis and Metaxas, and fled to the Dodecanese, which gave rise to the rumour that Italy had been a party to the insurrection.

This revolt gave a tremendous fillip to the movement in favour of a return to the monarchy as the only means of placing the interests of the nation above those of parties and individuals. In due course elections were held for a Constituent Assembly, which should decide the question of the regime, but the problem of the procedure to be followed revealed a difference of opinion between Tsaldaris and Condylis on the one hand, and Metaxas on the other. This was not unnatural, for Metaxas was a sincere Royalist who had never wavered in his allegiance, while the behaviour of Tsaldaris had been highly equivocal, and only two years had elapsed since Condylis had declared that if any attempt were made to restore the monarchy he would take to the hills to defend the republic. Tsaldaris and Condylis wished to leave the Assembly unfettered while Metaxas preferred that its members should be returned with the avowed object of restoring the monarchy. When the election took place in June, 1935, the policy of Metaxas won a percentage of votes out of all proportion to the number of seats which his followers obtained, and shrewd observers were convinced that before long the hesitating Tsaldaris would have his hand forced, which was precisely what took place.

It had already been arranged to hold a plebiscite on the restoration of the monarchy, and the Prime Minister wished to preserve the republican form until this had been done. Condylis, who was more closely in touch with public opinion than his timorous and pedantic chief, favoured the precedent of 1924, in which year, as has been shown, the change of regime was affected before the plebiscite, which subsequently confirmed it. As Tsaldaris refused to give way, he was forced by his masterful colleague to resign, and the monarchy was officially reinstated. The plebiscite was held on November 3rd, and some 97 per cent of the electorate voted for the restoration. No doubt the real minority was a very much larger proportion of the citizens, but, as Professor G. M. Trevelyan of the plebiscites of the *Risorgimento*, if "the plebiscite exaggerated it did not belie the opinion of the people". Six months after the return of the King a prominent Venizelist remarked, "Of course the plebiscite was faked, but to-day the King would get that majority on a free vote".

It is to be noted that King George II and his advisers were not enamoured of the idea of a plebiscite, and they were criticized in some Royalist circles for insisting upon one being held. Such criticism was really beside the point, for, in different circumstances from those prevailing in October, the King had earlier in the year given his consent to a plebiscite, and it was felt that both in Greece and abroad the worst possible impression would be created if it appeared that he had gone back on his word. Moreover, it was essential that he should not owe his return to military support, as would have been the case had he returned to Athens on the invitation of Condylis.

No sooner had the King reached the Greek capital from London than the wisdom of his action became manifest. He demanded an amnesty for all who had been implicated in the rising of the previous March, including Venizelos himself, and this Condylis was unwilling to grant. It has been stated that the King came to this decision as a result of certain conversations which he had in Paris, but there is every reason to suppose that his mind was already made up when he left London. Condylis refused to give way, and so within a few days of his return the King was compelled to dismiss the man to whom he appeared to owe his crown. On this account he naturally acquired a good deal of odium in ultra-Royalist circles, but this was surely undeserved. Condylis only declared himself a monarchist when he saw that public opinion was coming to favour a Restoration, and he was determined that the monarch should be a puppet, with himself as dictator. From the beginning he had played for his own hand, and King George in reality owed him nothing. It must be said in his favour that he took his dismissal with none too bad a grace, but as he died shortly afterwards it is impossible to say how long he would have continued to refrain from making trouble.

This action threw a good deal of light upon the late King's character, and had Mussolini studied the Greek monarch a little more carefully he might have been spared a very unpleasant surprise five years later. On first acquaintance King George II appeared somewhat reserved, and he was never one to talk if he had nothing to say. At the same time he was extremely level-headed, and the vicissitudes of his life made him a shrewd judge both of men and of situations. He was possessed of a keen sense of humour, and in spite of all that he suffered he never to the end betrayed a trace of bitterness. To his friends no man was ever more loyal. Eminently reasonable, once his mind was made up he was a very pattern of inflexibility, as both Condylis and Mussolini discovered to their cost. Because he lived in a West End hotel and went about a good deal socially, touching life at many points, King George was often depicted in the British Press as frivolous. Nothing could have been further from the truth. He had a very high sense of duty, and his conception of kingship was that of his grandfather, already quoted. To a friend who congratulated him on his recall to the throne he wrote that he hoped to "be able to prove worthy, as much as possible, of the new responsibilities". That was typical of the man. In addition to these natural instincts he had by 1935 studied from every angle the theory and practice of his royal profession, and he had acquired much invaluable advice during his exile from his relative King George V of England.

The dismissal of Condylis by no means put an end to the King's troubles. After the amnesty had been proclaimed elections were held, and these proved to be the most honest that the country had ever known. All the same they failed to give either of the leading parties, the Populists and the Liberals, as the former Royalists and Venizelists were now termed, a working majority, and as fifteen Communist deputies were returned the less scrupulous Liberals at once began to angle for their support. The King tried to get a coalition administration into office, and when his efforts in this direction proved a failure a non-party government was installed with first Demerdjes, and, after his death, Metaxas, at its head. When this had been done the Chamber went into recess for six months. The new ministry contained some able men, but it suffered from not having a free hand, for it was dependent upon a committee of party leaders, while the younger generation of Greeks, to whom it might have hoped to look for support, displayed as a whole no inclination to enter the political arena.

The consequence was an administrative paralysis which soon affected every sphere of the national life. Nor was this all, for Communist agitators were active up and down the country, and sporadic strikes, sometimes accompanied by bloodshed, were not infrequent. At the same time it was obvious that the party leaders, who were the cause of all the trouble owing to their refusal to form a coalition, had no following worth the name among the mass of the people. Matters came to a head at the beginning of August, 1936, when the Communists decided that the time was ripe for their intervention, and civil war on the Spanish scale became a distinct possiblity. From this Greece was saved by the King, who entrusted General Metaxas with full powers, and thus brought to an end a situation which had become intolerable. The Communists showed no fight once they were faced, and some fifty of them were deported to one of the islands in the Aegean. Thereafter King George was content to remain rather more in the background, though giving steady support to General Metaxas. It cannot, of course be denied that in acting as he did the King was responsible for a breach of the constitution, but the alternative was anarchy.

Although General Metaxas had for many years played a prominent part in Greek politics he had always been a soldier first and foremost. He was trained in Germany, and was highly thought of by the Great General Staff in Berlin in the days before the First World War, but when it came to a choice between a French and a German mission for his own country he chose the former. His was the brain behind the Greek strategy in the Balkan Wars, and, as we have seen, had his advice been asked before the Gallipoil expedition was undertaken the result of that unhappy venture might have been very different. Finally, his devotion to the Royal Family was profound, and every attempt to create a breach between him and his master failed.

Such was the background of revolution, war, and foreign intrigue against which must be set the success of King George II and his minister in securing a united country when the Italian ultimatum was delivered in October, 1940. In four short years they somehow contrived to harness to the service of the state that Greek quality of initiative and resource which is so common in business but is all too rare in politics. Their achievement was soon patent for all the world to see. Greek history, both ancient and modern, abounds in instances of στάσις and there can be little doubt but that Rome hoped that still one more example would aid her designs upon the neighbour with whom she had so recently promised to live at peace. Neverthless when General Metaxas and his master decided to accept the challenge in no quarter was there any tendency to Medize, and the Italians waited in vain even for the sight of that bright shield on Pentelicus which raised false hopes in the breasts of those other agressors, Datis and Artaphernes, two thousand five hundred years earlier. Less happy than Darius, the Duce did not find a Hippias to encourage the invader with illusions of facile successes, and the fact was the more remarkable in view of the divided state of Greek opinion for many a long year.

What followed belongs rather to the history of Greece than to an account of the Greek monarchy, though King George II personally was destined to undergo some very unpleasant experiences, both military and political, during the course of the Second World War and its aftermath. At first all went well, for not only did General Papagos resist every Italian attempt to invade Greece, but he carried the war on to Albanian soil, and by the spring of 1941 the capture of Valona appeared imminent. Then Germany perforce came to the aid of her ally, and the Bulgarian jackal made ready to join in the feast. In spite of the presence of a handful of British troops, Greece was over-run by the Germans, who soon extended their sway to the islands, including Crete. King George remained with his armies while any cohesion was left, and for his gallantry the Distinguished Service Order was conferred upon him by the King of England.

Then ensued one of those chaotic and somewhat discreditable periods which so often occur in Greek history immediately after deeds that have thrilled the imagination of mankind. General Metaxas had died on the eve of the German invasion, and he left no successor upon whom the King could rely. Instead, he was surrounded in Cairo, whither he and his government had betaken themselves after the loss of Crete, by a crowd of rather third-rate politicians most of whom tendered advice more in their own personal interest than in that of the national good. In these extremely troubled waters the representatives of the Allied Powers began to fish, and the confusion was rendered worse confounded by the fact that those of the same nationality by no means always pursued an identical policy: in this respect, it may be observed, the British were no exception. The situation was not improved by the mistaken Allied policy of supporting anyone who would oppose the Germans, irrespective alike of his origins and his aims. In this atmosphere the Greek armed forces gradually became demoralized, and one or two ugly incidents took place as a result of Communist activities.

For King George II and the Royal Family all this

was even more distressing than their exile in republican days: then the issue was at any rate clear, while now it had become confused by every kind of external consideration. The King spent most of his time in Cairo, much to the displeasure of the King of Egypt who resented the presence of another monarch in his capital; from time to time he visited London, where he always met with the most sympathetic reception both from King George VI and Mr. Winston Churchill, but on his return to the Near East he never found it very easy to get translated into action the decisions which had been taken in Whitehall. When, in the latter part of 1944 the Germans were compelled to evacuate Greece, it might have been supposed that the King's troubles were at an end, and that he would be able to go back to his own country, but this did not prove to be the case; civil war broke out, or rather the Communists, whom the Allies had so imprudently armed, made a desperate attempt to seize Greece by a *coup de main*, and there was heavy fighting before, with British assistance, the revolt was suppressed. It seemed as if the four years' achievements of the Metaxas regime had gone for nothing: the German and Italian occupation had ruined Greece materially, but even worse was the moral anarchy which the Communists had introduced.

All this time the British and American Governments had been exerting the strongest pressure upon King George not to return until order had been restored, and he had been most reluctantly compelled to give way. The argument that, if at all possible, a monarch should not become involved in a civil war which would involve the shooting of his subjects is a sound one, but there is some reason to suppose that certain Greek politicians of republican tendencies, aided by their British sympathisers, hoped that if the King's return could be indefinitely postponed it might never take place at all. In due course, however, a compromise was reached by which the Metropolitan of Athens, Archbishop Damaskynos, should act as Regent, and that in due course a plebiscite should be taken on the question of the return of the King. There was a recent precedent for a regency dating from the interval between the death of King Alexander and the restoration of King Constantine in 1920, while the plebiscite has become almost a convention of the Greek constitution, and it fitted in very well with the Allied Powers' affection for this procedure—that is to say as applied to others, for it has never been suggested that the views of the American, British, or Russian peoples as to the regimes they enjoy should be ascertained in this way.

The plebiscite was finally held on September 1st, 1946, and its result left no doubt as to the views of the Greek people, for 1,170,476 votes were cast in favour of, and 523,086 against, the return of the King. In consequence, King George came back to Greece once more with the assurance that a large majority of his subjects saw in him and in the principle he represented their only hope in the difficulties with which they were confronted. In the spring of the following year, 1947, however King George died, and there can be little doubt but that his death was hastened by the hardships and anxieties of the war years.

King George II was succeeded by his only surviving brother, Prince, now King, Paul. He had been offered the crown on the death of King Alexander twenty-seven years before, when he had declined with the words, "The throne does not belong to me; it belongs to my august father, King Constantine, and constitionally my eldest brother is his successor. Neither of them has ever renounced his rights". Now his chance had come, and the use which he has made of it is too wellknown to require description. As in the case of so many monarchs, there were those who doubted his ability to succeed in the difficult circumstances in which he ascended the throne, not least because he had not hitherto played any conspicuous part in politics. The sceptics were speedily confounded, and King Paul, with all the charm of his father, has known better how to work with his advisers. In his task he has been enormously helped by his consort, Queen Frederica, who is also his cousin once removed. Her courage during the Communist rising has become almost legendary in Greece, and it is safe to say that it is rare for any throne to be occupied by so well-beloved a King and Queen as is the Greek one to-day.

IV

MONARCHY IN CENTRAL EUROPE

Its Peculiar Nature—The German Background—Position of the Hohenzollerns—Kaiser Wilhelm II—His Failings as a Monarch—The Emperor and Hindenburg at Spa—Collapse of the German Monarchies—The Habsburgs—Their Government and Traditions—Metternich and His Legacy—The Emperor Francis Joseph and the First World War—The Serbian Menace—The Karageorgevitch Dynasty—Accession and Character of the Emperor Charles—His Bid for Peace—Mission of Prince Sixte—Its Failure—Verdict of Anatole France—Fall of the Habsburgs

MONARCHY in central Europe, that is to say to the East of the Rhine and in the valley of the Danube, has always been somewhat different in its nature from that which has distinguished it in the British Isles, France, Italy, and Spain. Its basis, namely the representation of the national, as opposed to sectional, interests has been for the most part the same, but circumstances have compelled it to safeguard these interests in a manner unknown in the western and southern countries of the European continent. It has been obliged to look for support to certain factors which, with the passage of time, gradually though imperceptibly, lost their importance, and so when the crises came the foundations of the various thrones gave way. The explanation of this is to be found in the contrasted historical development of the dynasties concerned.

In the first place the Crown was never identified with the nation as in England and France. The history of Germany can be searched in vain for an analogy to the rise of the Plantagenets and the Capets. The Hohenzollerns may appear to be an exception, but such is not really the case, for they were always Prussian rather than German in their outlook, and they were never prepared to sink Prussia in the Reich, as the Savoyards were content, to their own ultimate undoing, to allow the absorption of Piedmont in Italy. The German dynasties grew up among the ruins of the Holy Roman Empire, for the titanic struggle between Emperor and Pope begat principalities to the North, as well as to the South, of the Alps. In their struggle to establish the Imperial control over Italy the Hohen-staufen, particularly Frederick II, were compelled to make repeated concessions to the centrifugal influences in Germany, and when they fell it was too late to establish a centralized monarchy on the English or French pattern. Had the *Stupor Mundi* concentrated his attention on Germany rather than on Italy, he might well have done there what Henry II was doing in England and Philip II in France; but he preferred the Mediterranean to the Elbe, and the result of his choice was to postpone even the nominal unity of both Italy and Germany until the second half of the nineteenth century.

The consequence of this was the chaos that has marked German politics from that day to the present. In the place of a national monarchy with its feudatories, such as existed in England and France, there were literally scores of independent princelings, all of whom owed an allegiance, which every day grew more nominal and less real, to the Emperor. In the course of centuries circumstances, and the logical Latin mind of Napoleon I, greatly reduced their number, but by then it was too late to modify the character of German monarchy. Without any national basis, and ruling kingdoms and principalities that had no geographical or economic justification, the various dynasties naturally regarded their position in a different light from their contemporaries in London, Paris, and Madrid. They might ape the fashions of Versailles, even to the extent of maintaining official mistresses for ornament rather than for use, but the broad national and popular basis upon which the western monarchies rested was quite impossible for them to achieve.

This fact drove them to rely upon military support to an extent unknown to the West of the Rhine, and military they remained. The memoirs of English and French visitors to Germany in the eighteenth, and early nineteenth, century are full of references to the great display of uniforms to be found there, and some of the princelings, like the Landgrave of Hesse-Cassel, turned their dominions into establishments for the production and supply of mercenaries, which unpopular governments, like the Whig oligarchy in Great Britain, found extremely useful as police in times of crisis. A few of the German dynasties made themselves popular, either because they appealed to the particularist sentiments of those over whom they ruled, or because of the personal qualities of their members, but the principle which they represented aroused no great enthusiasm, and they were regarded as the countryman looks on the squire, not as the subject reverences his sovereign. On the other hand, there was equally no resentment against them, for they were not foreign, like the princes of contemporary Italy, and their short-comings were those of their fellow-countrymen. Apart from Prussia, the only exception to this state of affairs was to be found in Bavaria, where the Wittelsbachs ruled like the Stuarts; they stood for something more than a *schloss* and an army of toy-soldiers, and their reward was the love of their people, which even two World Wars did nothing to weaken.

Such was the background against which the new German Empire, the Second Reich, came into existence in 1871. Unity by general agreement had proved impossible in 1848, and after that failure it was clear that if the problem were to be solved at all it would only be by blood and iron. These methods were ruthlessly employed by Bismarck. Austrian influence in Germany was eradicated at Sadowa in 1866, and the treatment of Hanover was a warning to those states that were opposed to the policy of Prussia. The establishment of the German Empire was thus the last stage in the Prussian conquest of Germany, which Napoleon III, like his uncle quite unmindful of the true interests of France, had facilitated by his action in 1859 and 1866. In these circumstances, the Imperial monarchy naturally acted in the interests of Prussia, rather than in those of the Reich as a whole: in short, in assuming the Imperial crown the Hohenzollerns made no effort to shoulder the Imperial responsibilities, and the Treaty of Versailles was the price which the German people had eventually to pay for a dynasty that denied the principle upon which a long hereditary monarchy can rest. In effect, it was a bad day for the monarchical cause, for Germany, and for the world, when the Royal House of Prussia displaced the Habsburgs as the main factor in the politics of Central Europe.

From 1871 to 1914 the stock of the Hohenzollerns was undoubtedly priced too high, but since the end of the First World War it has equally certainly been unduly depreciated. The fact is that they were exceedingly able Kings of Prussia, but very indifferent German Emperors. Their short-sightedness is almost inconceivable, and was only equalled by their readiness to sacrifice all and every sort of principle for some temporary advantage once the Imperial crown was in their possession. First in Brandenburg, and then in Prussia, the Hohenzollerns, for generation after generation, pursued a consistent, patriotic, and truly monarchical policy, but as soon as the new dignity was theirs a frank opportunism became the order of the day. The German Empire, under their direction, reeled about like a man in his cups, and it was, as much as anything else, the uncertainty as to the course which would be pursued that precipitated the First World War.

One of the first acts of the new Empire was to intrigue with Thiers and Gambetta to prevent the restoration of the monarchy in France, and one of the last was to send Lenin and Trotsky to fan the flames of revolution in Russia. This reckless disregard of the principles upon which their throne was based was displayed by the Imperial Hohenzollerns in their attitude towards every problem that confronted them, and most of their ministers were no wiser than themselves.

The consequence was that the establishment of the German Empire in 1871 introduced a new disturbing factor into the world. The Napoleonic regime had been bad enough in this respect, but as it was founded by an adventurer, little could in any case be expected of it. The German Emperor, on the other hand, was a legitimate monarch, and he was surrounded by councillors who were supposed to be convinced monarchists, so there was the less excuse for what followed. The reason for this paradox was that in achieving the Imperial dignity the Hohenzollerns had been compelled to deny the principles upon which their position in Prussia was based, and their appetite grew for that upon which it had been fed. Wilhelm I became German Emperor over the dead body of Hanover, and having sacrificed one monarch to their ambition the Hohenzollerns naturally did not hesitate to apply the same methods elsewhere. The parallel with the House of Savoy will not pass unnoticed. So they industriously set to work sawing off the branch on which they were themselves seated, and when the crash came it unfortunately involved other dynasties, such as the Wittelsbachs, which had remained true to the old traditions of monarchy. Dog can never eat dog with impunity.

At the same time it must be admitted that Wilhelm I was never under any illusions as to his position. The old Emperor was by no means happy about the support which Bismarck insisted on giving to the French republicans, for he was a legitimist at heart, and it required all the sophistries of the minister, combined with the traditional jealousy felt by the Hohenzollerns for the Bourbons, to reconcile him to it. Wilhelm I also had the wisdom to realize that the Imperial crown might prove more of a curse than of a blessing, and he was extremely reluctant to assume it. The creation of Prussia had been the work of the Hohenzollerns, and they were admirably suited to rule a kingdom of that nature. Bismarck made them Emperors, and they proved unfitted to bear the burden which was imposed upon them. An Imperial outlook cannot be acquired in five minutes. As German Emperors the Hohenzollerns were always *parvenus*, and time to evolve a truly Imperial consciousness was denied them.

To give him his due, it must be recorded that Wilhelm I made no change in his behaviour after he became German Emperor, and his undoubted popularity among his subjects was very largely due to his unaffected simplicity. In many ways his position resembled that of Hindenburg in a later generation, and his whole outlook upon life was very different from that of his grandson. In private he was the typical *bourgeois*, as one illustration will serve to prove. A member of his household had occasion to see the Emperor one evening immediately after dinner, and asked the valet to announce him to his master. The servant asked the official to wait for a few minutes, as the Emperor was changing his clothes. To the comment that it was surely unusual for him to be doing so at that hour, the valet somewhat indignantly replied, "Do you imagine that he would go to the theatre in his new dinner trousers? It would not be like our old gentleman to be so extravagant".

The brief reign in 1888 of his son and successor, Frederick III, has furnished material for many speculations as to what would have happened had it been prolonged to the normal length, but from the historical standpoint it is only of importance in that it served to strengthen the determination of the Crown Prince to reverse his father's policy in every respect. In fact, the contrast between the two men was complete, physically as well as intellectually, and the moderation of Frederick was a repugnant to Wilhelm as was the Crown Prince's disabled arm, for which he blamed his mother. In any case there can be little doubt that Frederick III was the only member of the dynasty who had it in him to make a satisfactory German Emperor, and whether or not he would have fulfilled the expectations which had been formed of him, his death ushered in a period which can only be described as that of the twilight of monarchy in central Europe.

It is even now difficult to arrive at a true estimate of Wilhelm II. Although he has only been dead for a decade he belongs to history, but to such recent history that all the evidence necessary for a final judgment is not available. As one volume of memoirs succeeds another the balance, in the minds of all honest men, dips first to one side and then to the other, but it is quite impossible to say yet whether the credit or the debit side of the Emperor's account contains the greater number of entries. To arrive at even an approximately just estimate of his character it is first of all necessary to allow the Byzantine flattery which was lavished upon him in his earlier days, by no means only in his own country, to cancel out the ridiculous compaign of abuse to which he was subject during the period of the First World War.

Perhaps the shrewdest judgment ever passed upon him was that of the Emperor Francis Joseph, who said, "What a pity the German Emperor cannot hold his tongue! He talks too much and too often. It is better for us to be silent and let our ministers make the speeches". His temperament was that of the artist, rather than that of the statesman, and knowing that his nature was more akin to that of Hamlet than to that of Caesar, he was inclined to make up in words for what he lacked in deeds. There can also be little doubt that throughout his reign the Emperor believed that he had a definite mission to perform. "All his real self", Otto Hammann well observed in his *The World Policy of Germany*, 1890-1912, "was not contained in his boastful phrases and threatening gestures, as foreign critics believe; but, instead, he was under the delusion of being the instrument of Providence, a saviour of the whole world". In effect, his imagination controlled his judgment, with the result that his policy was vacillating, and there were continual complaints that no reliance could be placed upon him. It may even be that Wilhelm II knew in his own heart that he was not the mighty Imperator Rex that Europe believed him to be, and that he over-acted the part in an effort to convince himself that he really was what he seemed.

In his defence it must be admitted that he was wretchedly served by his ministers. Hohenlohe and Bülow are condemned out of their own mouths, and the other Chancellors were mere clerks, though on the whole somewhat more efficient ones than those who were to hold the office after the fall of the monarchy. The Germans are a great people, but, like the Italians, they lack the qualities essential for the production of statesmen. Now and again a man of the first rank (that is to say relative to other German statesmen) makes his appearance, but there is no regular supply of able men, and the second-raters are far inferior to their equivalents in, say, Great Britain. The reign of Wilhelm II was no exception to this rule, and what was lacking in the monarch was not supplied by the ministers. Holstein and Eulenberg exercised far too much influence, and the old maxims of Bismarck were ignored. In particular, the Iron Chancellor's policy of defending the German colonies on the battlefields of Europe was abandoned in favour of the creation of a navy, which alienated Great Britain; while Russia was allowed to drift into the French orbit, so that Germany was eventually faced with a war on two fronts. Finally, when hostilities did come, the ministers and generals. on whose demand every other interest had been sacrificed to the military, proved so incompetent that the war was lost. Like his subjects, the Emperor was the victim of the failure of the national character to produce statesmen.

It is now clear that the real responsibility for the fall of the German monarchy and the flight of Wilhelm II into Holland rested with Hindenburg, who subsequently admitted the fact. The history of what took place at Spa during the last hours of the Hohenzollern Reich is very well documented, and it shows a regime in complete dissolution, as was to be seen again in 1945; for when Germany cracks she cracks badly. The Emperor's decision to leave the country was not due to personal cowardice, but to the advice of Hindenburg and Gröner, given for reasons which are still somewhat obscure. During the war years Wilhelm II had become increasingly isolated, and in the hour of crisis he had no one to whom to turn, yet Brüning has himself stated that had the Emperor decided to face the revolutionaries they would have collapsed. As for Hindenburg, the memory of his action at Spa haunted him for the rest of his life, and it had an important bearing upon German political developments. Finally, to ease his conscience when he was dying he besought Hitler in his will to bring the Hohenzollerns back; not only was this injunction ignored, but the clause containing it was suppressed when the will was published.

The collapse of the Imperial throne may or may not have been a matter for regret, but it made the position of the other German dynasties impossible. The news that Wilhelm II had left the country so disheartened the monarchists everywhere that within the space of a few days there was not a throne left in the Reich, though subsequent events were to show that in the great majority of cases the republics which made their appearance were by no means wanted. In particular, the flight of the Emperor entailed the dethronement of the Wittelsbachs, who thus found themselves for the second time the victims of the Prussian Royal House, the previous occasion having been in 1871 when they were cheated of their proper rank in the new German Empire. While Crown Prince Rupprecht was leading home his defeated troops from France and Belgium in a manner befitting a soldier and a gentle-man, the overthrow of the Hohenzollerns emboldened a handful of revolutionaries to execute a *coup de main* at Munich, and his fate was that of the other dynasts.

It was not only convinced monarchists who had cause to regret these developments. The various dynasties were the reason for the existence of the different kingdoms and duchies, and once they had gone the centripetal influences were uncontrolled, with the result that the way was clear for Hitler and the Third Reich. The victorious Allies recked little for all this, and in encouraging republicanism in Germany in 1918 they made inevitable the Second World War.

If association with the Imperial Hohenzollerns proved most damaging to the other dynasties in the Reich, it was quite fatal for the House of Habsburg. Indeed, the argument may well be pushed even further, for surely Germany itself was a very definite loser when the control of central Europe passed from Vienna to Berlin. No less a prophet than Nietzsche spoke of "the uprooting of the German mind for the benefit of the German Empire", and Germany had lost her soul before she went down to disaster in 1918; how completely she had lost it the ensuing twenty years were to show. As if that were not enough she dragged the Habsburg monarchy down with her, and so precipitated a state of chaos in the whole of the Danube area which has defied every attempt to bring it to an end. Yet, with all their faults, and it would be idle to deny that they had their share of human failings, the Habsburgs possessed that Imperial outlook to which their Hohenzollern rivals never attained. Charles V spent his whole life in endeavouring to preserve the unity of Europe in an age when the centrifugal influences were growing stronger every day, and although he failed in the task his example was not lost upon his successors. In the seventeenth century the narrow-minded provincialism of some of the

German sovereigns loosed upon their country the horrors of the Thirty Years' War, and Germany became the battle ground of the French and the Swedes, whose aid was invoked by the enemies of the Emperor and the Empire. It is impossible to apportion exactly the responsibility for this catastrophe, but clearly the whole blame cannot be laid at the door of the Habsburgs, as has on more than one occasion been attempted by historians. When all is said and done, they were actuated by a desire to maintain European unity, and their justification is surely to be found in the misuse which their opponents, notably Prussia, made of their victory when the Habsburg writ no longer ran in the Reich.

Probably one reason why the work of the Habsburgs has been so unjustly depreciated is that few picturesque or romantic figures are to be found among the members of the dynasty, at any rate until the end of the nineteenth century, with the exception of Maria Theresa. Yet, slowly but surely, Emperor after Emperor spread the influence of civilization over vast areas that had never known it before, and as the tide of Ottoman invasion was rolled back one province after another was rescued from Asia, and incorporated in the general body of traditional European culture. Right up to the outbreak of the First World War this process continued, and the mark of Vienna is clear for all men to see beneath the waters of the new barbarism which of late years have submerged so much of south-eastern Europe. There may have been few outstanding personalities in the Imperial House, but there was continuity of policy in the administration, which was far more important, and as the two-headed eagle gradually replaced the Crescent humanity was very definitely the gainer.

It was the misfortune of the Habsburgs that

circumstances made them the object of attack when the French Revolution rendered nationalism and democracy popular throughout Europe. Their rule was not based upon either of the principles that had suddenly become fashionable, and so any disorder among their subjects, whatever the cause, was liable to be regarded elsewhere as the action of nations rightly struggling to be free. The course of events in Italy, in particular, during the fifty years which followed the Treaty of Vienna created a strong prejudice against Austrian rule in many parts of the world. In actual fact the Austrian occupation of Italy was dictated by military necessity, for if the Austrians had not garrisoned the peninsula the French would assuredly have done so, and thus the flank of the hereditary dominions of the Habsburgs would have been exposed. Strange as it may at first sight appear, the unification of Italy under the House of Savoy should have been a definite advantage to Austria, even though it meant the sacrifice of Venetia and Lombardy, for it closed one road to Vienna to the French, and rendered impossible any repetition of the strategy that had forced Francis II to sign the Treaty of Campo Formio in 1797; unhappily, however, the memory of old wrongs was too strong to allow either party to see where its true interest lay.

The greatness of a dynasty can to no inconsiderable extent be gauged by the quality of the men who serve it, and judged by this standard the Habsburgs must rank very high indeed, for they had Metternich as their minister. In this connection, however, it must be remembered that this remarkable man did not originate a policy, but rather applied the old principles of Habsburg rule to the problems by which he was confronted. Such being the case not a little of the praise must surely go to the Imperial House that had conceived the policy, though this in no way detracts from the credit of the statesman who showed himself so skilful in its application. Metternich would not have found it easy to serve the Hohenzollerns, and if he failed in the end it is at least arguable that it was not, as his contemporaries imagined, because he was behind the times, but rather because he was in advance of them.

Metternich shared to the full the traditional Habsburg belief in the unity of Europe, but he realized that if that unity were to be anything more than a fiction it must rest upon a new basis. Down to the Treaty of Westphalia in 1648 the assumption had been that if Europe was to be united it must be under the aegis of the Habsburgs as Holy Roman Emperors and heirs of the Caesars. This was the view of Charles V, but even he was unable to carry it wholly into effect, and his successors completely failed to do so before the opposition of France. Louis XIV endeavoured to achieve the unity of Europe under the French hegemony, and for a time he succeeded, but in the end the Bourbons failed as the Habsburgs had done before them. Napoleon tried along much the same lines, but he attempted to include in Europe the far-flung dominions of the Tsar, and his plans were buried in the Russian snows. The lesson, then, of three centuries of European history, from the accession of Charles V to the final overthrow of Napoleon, was that the unity of the continent could not be maintained on the basis of the acknowledged predominance of one Power over the others.

Metternich grasped this fact, and in place of the supremacy of one state he worked for common action by all. This was the idea behind the Holy Alliance, of which Metternich's biographer, Algernon Cecil, has written, "it was not particularly holy nor much of an alliance"; but the Austrian statesman's policy long survived the demise of that organization. From 1815 until 1848 the mainspring of politics in central Europe was to be found in Vienna, and European interests were never sacrificed for the temporary convenience of Austria. From 1870 to 1914 the part played by the Habsburgs in the earlier period was filled by the Hohenzollerns, and, at any rate after the dismissal of Bismarck, hardly a year went by during which the mailed fist of Prussia was not shaken in the face of one or other of the Powers. It is true that certain aspects of the policy of the Holy Alliance can hardly be defined, and they brought Canning into violent conflict with it on more than one occasion, but they in no way detract from the greatness of Metternich. He saw that the European Powers had certain common interests that transcended their particular interests, and he realized that unless the latter were subordinated to the former the continent of Europe would soon become the bear-garden to which the twentieth century was to see it reduced.

The policy of Metternich was inherent in the sovereignty of the Habsburgs, and he but gave it the form most suited to the age in which he lived. The catastrophe of his life was that his work did not survive, and it has been left to the present generation to appreciate his merit. First France and then Prussia put a sword into the machinery, which was not strong enough to resist such interference. Metternich was also unlucky in the Italian situation, where the monarchical principle had come to be so largely identified with alien domination. Above all, the rising tide of nationalism was against him.

The Emperor Francis Joseph was the pupil of Metternich, and for good and ill his long reign from 1848 to 1916 has left upon central Europe an influence that will be felt for many years to come. It was not in his nature to court publicity in the manner of Wilhelm II, and after the disasters of his early years he played no great part upon the European stage, but in his own dominions he attempted to put into practice that doctrine of the balance which he had learnt from his great mentor. He displayed uncommon shrewdness when he met the demands of Hungary, and it is a matter for regret that he did not adopt the same line with the Czechs, for had he been crowned King of Bohemia at Prague their autonomous movement might never have assumed an anti-dynastic form. It was the same mistake that Queen Victoria made with regard to Ireland, and King Alfonso XIII in respect of Catalonia.

The Emperor proved to the very end of his life that he had not forgotten the teaching of Metternich to avoid extremes, and one of his last acts was to refuse to agree to the establishment of a military dictatorship in Bohemia. Unfortunately his great age prevented him from being in a condition to exercise his authority at the very time when circumstances rendered it necessary that he should do so if the monarchy were to survive, that is to say when his German allies and his Hungarian subjects were joining hands to upset the balance upon which it depended. The Magyars had always pressed for an anti-Slav policy, and as German relations with Russia became strained in the early years of the twentieth century, it equally suited Berlin and Budapest to urge Vienna to strong measures against their common enemy, irrespective of the fact that the Habsburgs had always numbered millions of Slavs among their most loyal subjects. The Emperor resisted these arguments with all his ebbing strength, and had he been a younger man it is more than likely that he would never have given his consent to the declaration of war against Serbia in 1914.

At this point it will be as well to consider the then existing position in Serbia, the nucleus of the present Yugoslavia. Serbian history is one unbroken record of violence, and the events of the last few years have shown that in this connection at least there has been no breach with precedent. From its first stirrings for independence against the Turks at the beginning of last century Serbia was for nearly a hundred years torn between the feud of two rival dynasties, the Karageorgevitch and the Obrenovitch, of which the latter was slightly the more respectable if judged by western standards. Indeed, the founder of the Karageorgevitch line was a particularly repulsive scoundrel, who killed his mother by bonneting her with a hive full of bees, and his successors were little better. In June, 1903, the Obrenovitch line came to an end in circumstances of peculiar barbarity, when a number of officers burst into the palace at Belgrade and murdered the King and Queen in the small hours of the morning. The Queen, like Mary Tudor, had deceived herself into expecting an heir, and when one of the murderers had ripped her open with his sword, he plunged her nightdress into her body, to withdraw it, dripping with blood, with the exclamation, "Here is Queen Draga's baby". The royal bodies were then thrown out of the window, but the King was still alive and clutched at a bar, whereupon his fingers were cut off one by one. The man who opened the palace gates to the regicides was a young officer called Pera Zhivkovitch, who was afterwards the trusted adviser of successive Serbian and Yugoslav monarchs.

Peter I, the Karageorgevitch heir, took advantage of these atrocities to ascend the throne, and in consequence of the Balkan Wars he obtained for his country a considerable extension of her territory at the expense of the Sultan. Yet the malign destiny of Serbia was as active as ever. The Crown Prince, George, was at the best eccentric, and for some years Europe was continually being diverted by stories of his behaviour: on one occasion he was said to spend his spare time taking pot-shots at peasants from the palace windows, and on another he was reported to have drowned his tutor in the Save while they were out for a ride. On the other hand, it was whispered that he was not mad at all, and that these stories were put about by his younger brother, Alexander, to discredit him. However that may be, in 1909 George renounced his rights to the throne, and when Alexander succeeded his father he had the ex-Crown Prince shut up in a fortress, whence he recently emerged as a supporter of Marshal Tito. Alexander was no improvement on the rest of his line, though he maintained a greater appearance of respectability. In May, 1914, a month before the Archduke Francis Ferdinand was murdered at Serajevo, Alexander, then Crown Prince, visited the State printing works at Belgrade, when a compositor named Nadeljko Cabrinovitch was presented to him. The Crown Prince asked, "Are you the one?", and on receiving an affirmative reply said, "Well, good luck to you", and shook the man warmly by the hand. A few weeks later Cabrinovitch threw the first bomb at the Archduke. On February 2nd, 1930, under the dictatorship of King Alexander, the Crown Prince of sixteen years before, a memorial to Prinzip, the actual murderer of the Archduke, was officially unveiled at Serajevo. In October, 1934, King Alexander was himself murdered at Marseilles by a Croatian terrorist. As we have already seen dog does not eat dog with impunity.

History must not be read backwards: natural sympathy for the misfortunes of King Peter II during the Second World War, and disgust at the judicial murder of his supporter, General Mihailovitch, cannot blind one to the fact that the Karageorgevitch dynasty has little to recommend it even to the most convinced monarchist. The European significance of the revolution at Belgrade in 1903 was that the Obrenovitch line had been Austrophil, while the Karageorgevitch looked to St. Petersburg: no longer could Francis Joseph control his Slav subjects by means of a compliant King of Serbia, for under Peter I the more chauvinistic elements in that country were already looking forward to the union of all the southern Slavs under the Serbian crown, and to a revival of the Serbian Empire of the Middle Ages. Nor did the Serbs feel that they could afford to wait: in October, 1908, the old Turkish provinces of Bosnia and Herzegovina, long under Austrian occupation, were annexed to the Habsburg dominions, and if they settled down under the rule of Vienna then the very future of Serbia itself would be at stake, for the Dual Monarchy might become Triune, as it was already rumoured that the Archduke Franz Ferdinand wished; therefore he had to die, a sacrifice to the ambitions of a nation and its dynasty.

In spite of all this provocation, and even of the murder of his nephew, it is by no means impossible that had the Emperor Francis Joseph been ten years younger he would have seen that the right attitude to be adopted towards Belgrade was that summed up in the phrase *suaviter in modo*, but he was old and tired, the chauvinists carried the day, and the Peloponnesian War of modern Europe began.

In November, 1916, the long reign came to an end, and the young Emperor Charles succeeded to the throne. Few careers have been more tragic. The new monarch was inspired by all the best traditions of kingship, and he was very far from wishing that *guerre à outrance* which had become an obsession in Berlin, Paris, and, in certain circles, in London. It is often objected against him that he was weak, and failed to dominate events. There is, it must be confessed, a certain amount of truth in the second part of this charge, though it comes somewhat ill from those who have even more obviously failed to dominate events since his death. What is incontestable is that the Emperor stood for those very things which are essential to a stable Europe, that is to say the large economic unit (which the Austro-Hungarian Empire represented), a sane internationalism, and a bulwark against revolution. All these were swept away, with the Emperor Charles, in the flood of November, 1918, and mankind has been vainly struggling to get back to them ever since.

No estimate of the Emperor Charles would be complete without an account of his efforts to bring the First World War to a conclusion by negotiation, for that deserves to be remembered to his credit when the other events of his short reign have been forgotten. Whether his predecessor would have adopted the same line had he lived a little longer it is difficult to say, though there is some evidence to the effect that he might well have done so. From the beginning the Emperor Charles left no doubt as to his own sentiments, for in a proclamation which he issued on his accession he used the phrase, "I desire to do all in my power to end, as soon as may be, the horrors and sacrifices of the war". From a military point of view, too, the situation was favourable to one who held such opinions, for the prospect of a stalemate was becoming obvious to the most convinced chauvinist on either side. Various peace kites had already been flown, and in November, 1916, the Marquess of Lansdowne, though this fact was not known in Vienna, had laid a memorandum before the British Cabinet in which he suggested that the time had come to examine the possible bases for peace, and to make it plain that the Allies did not aim at the total destruction of the Central Powers.

This seems to have been the first definite step which any responsible statesman in any belligerent country had taken in the direction of a cessation of hostilities since the war began over two years before: there had been repeated declarations that the sword would not be sheathed until this or that had been done, but the actual war aims of the antagonists were largely a matter of conjecture. Of course Lord Lansdowne's proposal was unknown at home as well as abroad, and it is impossible to estimate what effect it might have had, for Mr. Asquith's administration was already tottering to its fall, and within a month it had ceased to exist—to be replaced by a government headed by Mr. Lloyd George, and pledged to a more vigorous prosecution of the war.

In Berlin the pacific disposition of the Austrian Emperor was viewed with considerable distaste, but it could not be ignored, and it was almost certainly responsible for the German offer to treat which was made on December 12th, 1916. The Central Powers— Germany, Austria-Hungary, Turkey, and Bulgaria— presented four identical notes in which they stated that they were willing to bring forward definite proposals, but also announced their intention of fighting to a finish if these were rejected. Whatever chance of success this step might have had in other circumstances, an extravagant speech by the German Imperial Chancellor, in which he threw all the blame for the outbreak of war upon the Allies, completely ruined. Such being the case, one may perhaps be pardoned for questioning the sincerity of the whole negotiation so far as Germany was concerned, for she may well have had no other object in view than to forestall a move on the part of Austria, and to place upon the Allies the onus of a refusal to discuss terms of peace. This, at any rate, was the interpretation put upon her action by those to whom the offer was addressed, and the impossibility of negotiating upon such a basis was demonstrated in speeches by Mr. Lloyd George, M. Briand, Baron Sonnino, and M. Pokrovsky. The suspicions of the Allied Powers were also voiced in their official reply on January 29th, 1917, when they declared, in addition, that there could be no peace without restoration and reparation.

A week after the Central Powers announced their willingness to enter into negotiations, the President of the United States, Mr. Woodrow Wilson, addressed a note to all the belligerents asking for a statement of their war aims as an essential preliminary to any approach to peace. It is clear that Mr. Wilson had decided to take this step before he was acquainted with the intentions of the Central Powers, and the State Department was at considerable pains to show that the two proposals were entirely unconnected. This fact was certainly appreciated by the governments concerned, though the general public in the Allied countries, which had no great love at that time for the President of the United States, showed a decided disposition to confuse the two events, and in private, if not in public, Mr. Wilson's note was widely denounced as neither more nor less than a deliberate attempt to second the efforts of the Central Powers. The only reply which this appeal elicited from the Allies was a paraphrase of that which was shortly afterwards sent to their opponents, and in it they declared that "their objects in the war will not be made known in detail with all the equitable compensations and indemnities for damages suffered until the hour of negotiations". It was, however, stipulated that the Turk should be expelled from Europe, but no mention was made of the retrocession of Alsace-Lorraine to France.

This interchange of notes, though it led to no definite result, cleared the air to some extent. It showed that Germany was not ready to treat upon any basis to which her enemies would agree, and that the Allies were not prepared to accept the mediation of a neutral, for although Mr. Wilson had not actually offered his services in that capacity, it was clear that they were available if desired. On the other hand, the reticence of the Allies suggested either that they were not in complete agreement with regard to their aims, or that these were subject to negotiation. The Emperor Charles felt that in either case there might be a chance for him to secure a settlement, and so, in the early days of February, 1917, he got into communication with his brother-in-law, Prince Sixte of Bourbon-Parma, with this end in view.

Prince Sixte was at that time serving with the Belgian army because no Bourbon was allowed with the French forces, and he readily obtained the permission of King Albert to co-operate with the Austrian Emperor. He was then informed of the terms upon which his brother-in-law considered peace to be possible. These were: firstly, the conclusion of a secret armistice between Austria-Hungary and Russia in which the question of Constantinople was not to be made an issue; secondly, the restoration of Belgium and of Alsace-Lorraine—the latter, incidentally, a concession which had not yet been demanded by the Allies themselves; and thirdly, the formation of a southern Slav monarchy which should include not only Serbia, Montenegro, and Albania, but Bosnia and

Herzegovina as well. It should be noted in connection with these suggestions that there was at that time no idea in the mind of the Austrian Emperor of concluding a separate peace; all that he intended to do was to explore the ground, and when he had arrived at a general understanding with the Allies, he proposed to place before Germany, Bulgaria, and Turkey certain definite recommendations based upon it. Great Britain, France, and Russia were, it may be added, each precluded from making a separate peace by an agreement of September 5th, 1914, to which Italy became a party in November of the following year.

As a French subject Prince Sixte naturally laid his brother-in-law's proposals before the President, then M. Poincaré, in the first place, and he in his turn communicated them to M. Briand, who was both Premier and Minister for Foreign Affairs. The two Frenchmen agreed that they might well form a basis for negotiations, but they warned Prince Sixte that Italy would be the chief obstacle to any understanding. As a result of two interviews with M. Poincaré the Prince went to Vienna, where he saw the Emperor in the latter part of March. Unfortunately in the interval two events took place which were destined to bring about the failure of the negotiations, namely the outbreak of the Russian Revolution and the fall of the Briand administration. The first of these soon weakened Russia to such an extent that the jingoistic elements in Berlin and Vienna once more became convinced, with considerable justification it must be admitted, that the victory in the field which had seemed beyond their capacity to achieve at the end of 1916 was again within their grasp, while the second resulted in the installation as Premier and Minister for Foreign Affairs of M. Alexandre Ribot, a man whose capacity never rose above mediocrity and generally failed to attain it. However, in spite of these drawbacks Prince Sixte continued his mission, and he was assisted by the fact that as the spring of 1917 was exceptionally late, and the Germans executed a retirement in the West, there was a comparative lull in the fighting.

On the return of Prince Sixte from Vienna, where he informed the Emperor of the attitude of France, it was decided to acquaint the British Government with what was afoot. Accordingly, M. Ribot told Mr. Lloyd George of the Austrian proposals, and the British Prime Minister promised complete secrecy with the reservation that he felt himself bound to mention the offer, though somewhat surprisingly not to mention the details, to King George V. As evidence of the relations existing between Vienna and Berlin, it is to be noted that the chief reason why Prince Sixte insisted upon such complete secrecy was the fear that if news of the proposals reached Germany the Austrian Emperor would be murdered at official German instigation within a week. On April 18th, 1917, Prince Sixte had an interview with Mr. Lloyd George, in which the Welshman showed himself extremely sympathetic, but, like M. Poincaré, he feared that Italian ambitions would prove an insurmountable obstacle, for Italy was supposed to be demanding the Trentino, Dalmatia, and all the islands in the Adriatic that belonged to Austria-Hungary. At this point, however, it was discovered that the Italian Government, behind the backs of its allies, was already engaged in a separate engagement with Vienna on the basis of the cession of the Trentino alone, and in these circumstances there seemed to be no special reason why London and Paris should be unduly careful of Italian susceptibilities.

Prince Sixte, therefore, came to England in May, and remained there until the first week in June, during which time he saw King George V and had several conversations with the Prime Minister. The position then was that both the Emperor Charles and Mr. Lloyd George were extremely anxious to come to terms, but the Emperor had become so thoroughly convinced of the impossibility of inducing his German ally to listen to any proposals for bringing the war to an end that he was now prepared to negotiate a separate peace for his own dominions. On the other hand, M. Ribot was at best luke warm, though whether it was his head of his heart that was at fault is a problem which may never be solved. As for Count Czernin, the Austro-Hungarian Foreign Minister, he could not be trusted, though his master was not yet aware of the fact. The truth was that Czernin was in close contact with the militarists in Berlin, and he took care to serve their interests with far greater zeal than he did those of his own monarch. On one occasion, indeed, he actually proposed that Austria should become a definite vassal of Germany, and when it was objected that the Emperor Charles would never agree to this, he remarked: "Leave it to me. I will soon bring him as far as that". Lastly, the King of Italy refused to pay a visit to the Western Front, where it had been hoped to have arranged a meeting with the King of England and the French President at which the three Heads of States could have exchanged views on the Austrian proposals.

Mr. Lloyd George suggested that he and the French Premier should go to Vienna, but this was far too pacific a move for Ribot's liking, and he summarily rejected it. So evident, however, was the British Government's determination to make a separate peace with Austria, if such a thing were at all possible, that, in view also of the known opinions of the French President, Ribot felt compelled to do something, and, after a good deal of negotiation between London and Paris, Great Britain and France proposed certain terms to Austria at the beginning of August, 1917. These comprised the cession of the Trentino to Italy, and the establishment of Trieste as a Free Port, while in exchange Austria-Hungary was to receive Silesia, Bavaria, and Poland within the frontiers of 1772. In other words, she was again to be the predominant power in Germany, and a bulwark against the danger that threatened from the East, though this was no longer the Turk, but the rising tide of Bolshevism.

Unfortunately this step was taken too late, and the course of the actual fighting was such as to render the very continuance of negotiations impossible. A British offensive had been launched on the Western Front at the beginning of July, while the delivery of the Allied note almost coincided with an Italian attack that came within an ace of breaking through the Austrian resistance. This last threat was a very useful weapon in the hands of Czernin and the Pan-Germans, who were able to quote it in support of their argument that only the help of Berlin could prevent the Austrian counter-attack resulted in the Italian defeat at Caporetto, and British and French troops were hurried to the Piave, where, for the first time, they came into actual conflict with the armies of Austria-Hungary. The vicious circle was complete, and Ribot, still Minister of Foreign Affairs though no longer Prime Minister, closed the door upon any further negotiations in a speech of quite exceptional bitterness. In the following year there was another exchange of polemics, this time between Clemenceau and Czernin, and the air was thick with such charges as "*Monsieur Czernin a menti*", and "*Herr Clemenceau hat gelogen*". Czernin even threatened to commit suicide, but omitted to carry out his threat. Once, when he was talking in this vein, a visitor laid a revolver on the table, and went away, "but", he afterwards related, "I waited some time on the stairs without hearing him fire".

Finally, it was of this episode that Anatole France wrote: "No one will ever persuade me that the war could not have been ended long ago. The Emperor Charles offered peace. There is the only honest man who occupied an important position during the war, but he was not listened to. In my opinion his offer ought to have been accepted. The Emperor Charles has a sincere desire for peace so everybody hates him. Ribot is an old scoundrel to have neglected such an occasion. A King of France, yes, a King would have taken pity on our poor people, bled white, attenuated, at the end of their strength. But democracy is without heart, without bowels. A slave of the powers of money, it is pitiless and inhuman".

This incident has been narrated at length partly, as has been said, because it is essential to an understanding of the character of the last Austrian Emperor, and partly because it well illustrates the part which a sovereign could play in international affairs as recently as the second decade of the present century. In the following year, 1918, the Austro-Hungarian Monarchy collapsed in consequence of the defeat of the Central Powers, and the Habsburgs ceased to be numbered among the Reigning Houses of Europe.

SOME OTHER MONARCHIES

It was once well said of the *ancien régime* in France that it was a despotism tempered by epigrams, while in Russia it was a despotism tempered by assassination. The second observation was unquestionably true, and only the history of the Karageorgevitch dynasty is in any way comparable with that of the House of Romanoff in the eighteenth and early nineteenth centuries. The succession to the throne was most irregular, and Alexander I, the protagonist of the Holy Alliance, owed his crown to the murder of his father, to which it is by no means certain that he was not an accessory.

In effect, to understand the working of the monarchical system in Russia it is necessary to remember that she was not the most easterly of the European Powers but the most westerly of the Asiatic states. As everywhere in the Orient, power was remote: that close touch between rulers and ruled, whatever the regime, which is the pre-requisite of success for government in Europe does not exist in the East, least

of all in Russia. While the western states were slowly
emerging from the Dark Ages, and finding in throne
and altar their inspiration, Russia was subject to the
remote and barbaric rule of the Mongols. So long as
their subjects paid their taxes and gave no sign of
exercising any initiative all was well; but let them
display any independence of thought and action, and
down came the terrible horsemen of the Golden Horde
to wreak their ghastly vengeance. The memory of
those days lasted throughout the centuries of Tsarist
rule, and many would say that it is far from dead even
now.

Russia, too, was cut off from the civilizing influences
of the West. "The barbarous populations of the
Russian plain were far withdrawn", wrote Mr.
H. A. L. Fisher, "from the thoughts, ideals, and
activities, which, during the Middle Ages and afterwards, moulded the life of the Latin and Teutonic
races. . . . The vast inclement country, alternately
parched by the summer sun, or buried under a pile of
arctic snow, constituted a world sufficient for itself,
uninviting to others". In consequence, however, of
the growth of her influence in the international sphere
Russia in the eighteenth and nineteenth century
became increasingly immersed in the affairs of the
West particularly in those of Germany, and particularly was this so after the overthrow of Napoleon. If,
however, Russian armies reached Paris, the ideas of
the French Revolution penetrated Russia, where in
certain circles they met with a ready acceptance.

The Tsars did not pursue any consistent policy
where this movement was concerned. Alexander I was
liberal in his youth, but in latter years he acted on very
different principles, while his brother and successor,
Nicholas I, made no pretence of sympathy with
progressive ideas. Alexander II was inclined to a more

liberal policy, and during his reign, 1855-1881, serfdom was abolished. By this time, however, Nihilism had established a hold upon the revolutionary elements, and in 1881 the Tsar was himself murdered in the streets of St. Petersburg. Not unnaturally, his successor, Alexander III, adopted repressive measures during his short reign of thirteen years. Such was the position when the last Tsar, Nicholas II, came to the throne in 1894.

His character is not easy to assess. He was certainly not the bloodthirsty tyrant which he was so often depicted—had he been he would in all probability have died peacefully in his bed as Tsar of All the Russias. He was also extremely well-intentioned as he proved when on his initiative the first International Peace Congress was convoked at The Hague in 1899. His real demerit as a sovereign was his weakness and his dependence upon others, chiefly upon the Tsarina, who was not a good counsellor. Whether the Russian monarchy would have been overthrown had it not been for the First World War is a moot point, but that it would not have been overthrown so easily may be stated with confidence. During the course of it Nicholas II became completely detached from his subjects, while the gross incompetence displayed by every department of the administration rapidly reduced to vanishing-point the traditional respect for the throne.

Nor was this all, for the extremely severe casualties which the Russian armies suffered in 1914 and 1915 were by no means without their political repercussions. The best of the regimental officers were killed, and they were just the men who would have rallied to the monarchy in the hour of danger. When the crisis came the Tsar had no one individual nor any section of the community to which he could turn, and so, as Kipling sang,

.... this Kingdom and this Glory and this Power and
    this Pride
Three hundred years it flourished—in three hundred
    days it died.

To what extent this was the fault, and to what the
misfortune, of the last Tsar, is likely to be canvassed
for many a long year.

In the North-West of Europe there are three nations,
namely Denmark, Norway, and Sweden which have
never experienced republican rule, and in which there
is no republican party worth the name, yet they are
all three among the most progressive countries of
Europe.

Proof of their devotion to the principle of monarchy
is proved by the action taken by Norway in 1905,
when she severed her constitutional bond with Sweden.
Of all the European nations Norway is, one would
have thought, the most suited for a republic, "Here",
a distinguished historian has written, "is a people of
peasants, merchants, fishermen, and sailors, free from
those abrupt differences of wealth and station which
are so painfully evident in most European states, and
preserving in its geographical isolation and archaic
simplicity of life the high spirit of independence
appropriate to a mountain race". After a long and
bitter constitutional struggle Norway succeeded in
severing the connection with Sweden which had been
forced upon her to suit the convenience of European
diplomacy ninety-one years before. The Norwegians
agitated for the creation of a Norwegian Ministry of
Foreign Affairs, for Norwegian consuls, and for a
Norwegian flag. The King of Sweden refused to make
the necessary concessions, and in due course found that
he could not obtain a Norwegian ministry. When this
stage had been reached the Storthing in Christiania,

as Oslo was then called, declared that the royal power had become inoperative, and that the union with Sweden under one King was dissolved.

A section of Norwegian opinion, headed by the novelist Bjornson, was in favour of the establishment of a republic, but it soon transpired that the republicans were divided, for some advocated a regime on American lines with a strong President, while others preferred the French or Swiss model, in which the Head of the State would be a mere figurehead. The monarchists, on the other hand, were united, while they also had the advantage that the Norwegians had been given to understand that a monarchy would be more acceptable than a republic both in London and in Berlin, and the new state required all the outside support it could get. A King, moreover, would imply dynastic alliances, and these would afford additional security. So the crown was offered to, and accepted by Prince Charles of Sweden, who ascended the throne as King Haakon VII. How deeply he endeared himself to the Norwegian people the events of the Second World War were to show.

Denmark and Sweden have, during the twentieth century, been equally happy in and with their sovereigns, and they provide a striking example of the fact that monarchy and liberty can agree very well together.

The nineteenth century witnessed the rapid decline of Portugal. The Peninsular War caused widespread damage, and the loss of Brazil, which took place soon after its close, was a further severe blow. For the next hundred years the annals of Portugal bear a striking resemblance to those of Spain, as described on an earlier page. There was a dynastic division along not dissimilar lines, which, as in the neighbouring kingdom, led to civil war and then to the enthronement of that branch of the Royal House which was forced to look to the Left for support; there was an imported constitution which was quite unsuited to the national needs, and which no one proved capable of working successfully; and there was a growing moral and spiritual anarchy which successive administrations proved unable or unwilling to repress.

In 1889 King Carlos succeeded to the throne, and in the early years of the present century he determined to stop the rot, and in consequence he gave full power to Senhor Franco, a man of outstanding ability and integrity. Whether or not this step would have proved successful it is impossible to say, for in February, 1908, King Carlos and the Crown Prince, Luis, a young man of singular promise, were murdered in the streets of Lisbon. He was succeeded by his younger son, King Manuel II, who proved to be very much under the influence of his mother. An attempt was made, as in Spain after the fall of General Primo de Rivera, to get back to normal political life, and Senhor Franco was dismissed. All that happened was that the old maladministration was resumed, and the throne became implicated. In 1910 a republic was established because the monarchy suddenly collapsed, for there is no other way of describing the fall of King Manuel II.

It only remains to add that in 1919 there was a Royalist rising which would in all probability have led to the restoration of the monarchy, but for reasons which have never been satisfactorily explained the King refused to return, and the movement came to nothing. King Manuel II was the last of his, the junior, branch of the House of Braganza, and since his death the heir to the throne has been Dom Duarte, who, with the approval of Dr. Salazar, has of late years come to reside in Portugal.

Of the Netherlands it can be truly said that the state is the creation of the ruling dynasty, the House of Orange-Nassau. If nations which have no history are happy, then so are Royal Families, and there have been no differences of the least importance between the Dutch dynasty and the Dutch people during the present century. In 1890 Queen Wilhelmina succeeded her father, King William III, and she reigned until 1949 when owing to advancing years she abdicated in favour of her daughter, the present Queen Juliana. When her country was over-run in the Second World War the Queen, like the Kings of Greece and Norway, displayed the greatest courage; she went into exile with her ministers; and returned in the hour of victory amid the applause of her subjects.

As for Belgium, much the same could have been said of her and her Royal Family until a comparatively recent date, when, unfortunately, events began to take a very different turn. The reigning dynasty is not, of course, of local origin, but is a branch of the House of Saxe-Coburg and Gotha, of which the Prince Consort, the husband of Queen Victoria of England, was a member. When Belgium in 1830 broke away from the Netherlands, to which she had been united by the Treaty of Vienna fifteen years before, the Powers had endowed her with a King in the person of Prince Leopold and Saxe-Coburg and Gotha, who took the title of Leopold I. He and his successors speedily settled down in their adopted country, and they proved to be competent and patriotic monarchs, even if the morals of King Leopold II left in some respects a good deal to be desired.

When Belgium was invaded by the Germans at the beginning of the First World War the reigning monarch, King Albert, withdrew with his army, although Brussels fell into the hands of the enemy, and he did not return to the capital until victory had been won. It was due to the fact that his son and successor, King Leopold III, did not pursue the same policy in the Second World War that the recent dynastic crisis in Belgium has been due.

In this connection it is impossible wholly to ignore the character of the monarch himself. From his mother, a member of the House of Wittelsbach, he seems to have inherited certain *traits* which are in marked contrast with those that have distinguished the Coburgs, and the sudden death of his wife, Queen Astrid, in a particularly tragic motor accident undoubtedly left a deep impression upon him. Nor was this all, for in spite of what happened in August, 1914, the King appears to have believed that it would be possible to preserve Belgium neutrality in the event of a Second World War. At any rate he was by no means disposed to participate in military discussions with Great Britain and France, an attitude which naturally roused criticism in certain quarters. King Leopold III was thus already the object of some suspicion even before the storm broke.

When the Germans invaded the Low Countries in May, 1940, these apprehensions were for a time forgotten; the King took his place in the field as commander-in-chief of the Belgian army, and co-operated with his British and French allies. Then came the sudden capitulation of the Belgian forces, of which one of the terms was that King Leopold become a prisoner of the Germans in his palace of Laeken. At once the flood-gates of criticism were opened, and in a broadcast the French Prime Minister denounced the King as little better than a traitor. Among Belgians themselves opinion was equally divided, and there was a considerable school of thought which held the view that King Leopold should not have constituted himself a prisoner, but should have accompanied his ministers to London as the Queen of the Netherlands had done.

In problems such as this it is always impossible to dissociate the personal and the political. In due course, while still in captivity, the King made a morganatic marriage, and, on various scores, this roused widespread resentment among his subjects. It is true that in the later stages of the war the Germans removed him from Belgium altogether, but this did little to restore his popularity, and by this time a large section of Belgian opinion had become, by no means wholly spontaneously it may be observed, definitely hostile to him.

Between the close of the Second World War in 1945 and the summer of 1950 the problem of King Leopold and his return to the throne was a running sore in Belgian politics. A temporary arrangement was made by which the King lived in exile in Switzerland, while his duties were performed in Brussels by his brother Charles, as Prince Regent, but between the partizans on both sides the bitterness continued to grow. On the whole the Flemish were for the King, while the Walloons called for his abdication in favour of the Crown Prince Baudouin. As these were, in any case, old lines of cleavage there were occasions when it looked as if nothing could prevent an appeal to force.

The final settlement did more credit to the common-sense of the Belgian people than to the statesmanship of its leaders. A narrow majority at the polls induced the Catholic Party to hold a plebiscite on the King's return, and although this only showed a small majority in his favour he at once came back to Brussels. This was bad enough, for it was clear from the moment of his arrival that he would be the mere nominee of a faction, and King of the Belgians only in name, but worse was to follow. The leaders of the Socialist Party, one of the most respectable and constitutionally-minded organizations in Europe, with M. Spaak at their head, proceeded to incite their followers to mount the barricades in the best style of 1848.

For a day or two it looked as if the most orderly nation in Europe was about to be rent by civil war, and then, on the very brink of the abyss, the forces of moderation asserted themselves. It was decided that King Leopold III should remain on the throne for a space, but that all the royal prerogatives should be exercised by the Crown Prince, who should then succeed him. This procedure has been followed, and King Baudouin now occupies the throne. It is to be hoped that this settlement will finally take the monarchy out of Belgian party politics, but bitter feelings have been roused, and it would be idle to pretend that they will be easily allayed. Much will depend upon the new King himself.

INDEX